For Mary Teresa

Merry Christmas!
2000

the connemara bus

Ann Milholland Webb
who found her way
home at last!

Hugh Ryan
"THE BUS DRIVER"

Love "2000"
Eddie

The Connemara Bus

By
Ann Milholland Webb

Leathers Publishing
4500 College Blvd.
Leawood, KS 66211
Phone: 1 / 888 / 888-7696

ISBN: 1-58597-010-7

Library of Congress Catalog Card No. 99-75575

Leathers Publishing
4500 College Blvd.
Leawood, KS 66211
Phone: 1 / 888 / 888-7696

dedication

andrew james ferguson,
loving husband, father, grandfather,
trusted and reliable friend and neighbor;

and to

james joseph mcholland,
my daddy and my pal; a true irishman,
who never had the opportunity to come home,
until now.

ACKNOWLEDGMENTS

My thanks to Waltons Musical Instrument Galleries Ltd., Dublin, Ireland, for copyright permission to include the words of the song entitled "The Connemara Bus" in this book.

In addition, my heartfelt thanks go to:

The Ryan family, for entrusting the handling of their written lives to my care; especially to Hugh for inspiring me to write the story and believing in me. My added thanks to your generosity for the untold hours you selflessly dedicated to driving, talking, sharing, and editing. You exemplify, in the truest sense, the meaning of being a Connemara gentleman — an Irish gentle man;

Freda, first for living your story, then for collecting, sorting and editing it. You are to be commended for your part in molding and helping form such a wonderful group of human beings called the Ryans;

Liam for getting me started on this long road to wherever we are all going together; and to Connie, Anne, Margaret, Freda and Anthony; and all of your loved ones, for rounding out such a beautiful family;

My love to Debbie, Paul, Deborah, and Gillian for welcoming me into your home. And a special hug to Andrew, his great-grandfather's namesake, for sharing secrets with me.

I also owe many, many thanks to:

My own family members who help me arrive safely at all of my destinations. My love to Jim, who sees me through my daily crises; Janice, who tends to my emotional crises; her husband Kraig, who can talk me out of my corners; and their son, Graham, my ray of sunshine and loving grandchild;

My late husband, Bob, inadvertently delivered me to the doorstep of the Ryan family. His love and encouragement in all of my endeavors were always my rock;

My brother, Dennis, who diligently saw that I got to my appointed rounds and then walked me through my emotional mine fields;

My dear friend, Barbara Funk, who abundantly shares her wisdom with me, but only after gently and carefully infusing her professional and critical expertise into it. You can send me back to Ireland anytime you want. Thanks, Barb!

Also I add my appreciation to the relatives, friends, and neighbors who shared their time and memories of Andrew and Daisy Ferguson: Pat O'Halloran, Brendan Ferguson, Frank O'Toole, Roger Finnerty, Tim and Maureen Molloy.

chapter one

I DO NOT BELIEVE that death takes a holiday when I board a plane. It takes us when it is our time to go. However, I have never had a great interest in going when it is the pilot's time to go.

I glanced around at the snoozing passengers and wondered what it would be like to be able to sleep on an airplane. I think the airlines should not charge me full fare to fly, because I never let all of my weight down in my seat — and I shift my weight from one hip to the other every five minutes.

The flight from Kansas City to Boston passed by without incident. The young man next to me talked non-stop about his wife, his business and his baby. I wish he had continued on as my seat partner for the transcontinental flight. Who knows, he might even have talked me to sleep. The sleeping tablets I took hadn't done the trick.

None of the people around me appeared to be the least bit interested that my husband was dead — or that this was the first time I had ever flown alone. Bob used to tell people that his only fear of flying was getting gangrene in his arm next to me.

It took me eight months to be able to say the words, "My husband is dead," without screwing my face in a little knot, causing tears to splash and my nose to drip. I can say those words now, but every once in a while my emotions still sneak up and bite me.

Early in our marriage, Bob and I delineated the things I liked to do and the things he liked to do. The rest of the tasks were split between us for balance. It worked for us. Since his death, I have learned to license a car, change furnace filters, file an income tax return, put out the trash for collection. I finally got the hang of the last one by listening to the trash truck drive by several times without stopping. I have also had the car serviced — almost always on time. And I have learned to deal with that "ding, ding, ding" that tells me I need to fill the gas tank. I had never even heard that sound before because that, too, was a Bob job. For other funny noises I can't identify, I call my son.

My baby brother, Dennis, gave me an ironclad guarantee that if I would visit him in Ireland, I would go home with a renewed outlook on life. His persistence and last telephone call finally wore me down. It took every ounce of my courage to tell him that I would do it. I told myself, "You'd better get a grip, girl, because from now on, you are on your own."

Dennis and I have always been good friends, in spite of the big gap in our ages. But still, we are so different.

Dennis quit high school soon after he had earned enough credits to graduate. Speaking only self-taught German, he received the remainder of his education in Germany. At last count, I think he had completed five degrees, including a German law degree. He speaks 11 languages and worked his way through college as an instantaneous interpreter, sitting in the basement of conferences and talking to the people upstairs wearing headphones.

I speak English, but not all that well; pig Latin, when called upon; and a few select words of profanity. I am still working on my first master's degree. In some fashion or another, I have been attending school for over 60 years.

I was the baby of the family for 18 years until Dennis pushed me out of my spot. He claims he always felt like the tag end of the family instead of a part of it. Consequently, he went to Europe at the age of 18 and never returned again to live in America.

No matter where he has lived, he has always welcomed our visits. In the past, he vacationed with us as a family and is now encouraging the tradition even though I am no longer a couple.

When I agreed to visit Dennis this time, I told him I did not want to go anywhere we had been with Bob and the kids. And since this was probably going to be my last visit, I suggested we research our roots in the west of Ireland, near County Mayo.

He agreed to all of my rules and rented a townhouse in Galway — clear across the country from where he lives in Dublin.

I reached up and turned off the overhead reading lamp that might be keeping someone else awake. I knew from experience that having the light on or off wouldn't make any difference to me. I tried to get comfortable so I could let my mind ramble for the next six hours.

The woman next to me made it quite clear that she did not want her seat partner to invade her space. She very smartly guarded against this by not bathing or shampooing for a week or so.

Even though my travel agent had assured me I had an aisle seat, I nestled down against the window with my postage-stamp-sized pillow, fully aware that my eyes would never close.

I spent the next six hours trying to decide whether I wanted to go on living or not. My daddy would have been so disappointed to know I was thinking of not fighting for something that was worth the struggle. He had been a fighter and had taught me to be a fighter.

I had been lucky enough to find a husband who encouraged me to be anything I wanted to be and do anything I wanted to do. He picked up right where Daddy left off on that May evening when Daddy placed my hand in his. With our exchange of "I do" promises, I went from being Jimmie's daughter, or "Pal," as he most frequently called me, to being Bob's wife, Ann.

Names are only secondary labels for me, because I have always been my own person and have always had a good sense of my own being — until now.

I was handling Bob's death a whole lot better than I had Daddy's. It seems to be easier, because I have gone through what the experts deem to be the appropriate grieving process for Bob, but I had never done that for Daddy. I tucked him away in a special little place deep in my heart to be dealt with later. After 15 years, he is still there, waiting.

I wish Daddy had been able to visit Ireland before he died — to visit what he called his homeland. He was so proud of his heritage.

Daddy had his own little rituals that reminded him of his ties to his homeland. He kept his own little squat, cream-colored crockery jug on the mantel above the fireplace. The brown neck and handle and most of the burgundy-colored wax sealer clung to the area that had originally sealed the cork. It still gripped a little piece of green ribbon under the identification seal that had been embossed in the wax. It looked like petrified honey, laden with dust.

Daddy wasn't a drinking man, but once a year, during the Christmas holidays, he would take down the jug, pull the cork and "wet his whistle." They couldn't have been very big sips because the contents of the quart jug provided moisture for his whistler throughout all the years of my young life.

Daddy willingly shared his time, his love, his spirit for adventure, but one of the few things he didn't share was his crúiscín lán, which is Irish for a full little jug. I don't know where Daddy got his little jug of Irish whiskey, and I don't know that he wouldn't have shared had he been asked, but it seemed to be such a personal ritual that I don't remember anyone ever asking.

I have not cried for Daddy since the day of his funeral. I felt no anger toward him for leaving me, for I know he wouldn't have done it willingly. I never tried to bargain with God, nor had I gone through any of the other steps that counselors and therapists seem to think so necessary for healthy healing. All I know is that I still miss him and I miss him a lot.

When Daddy died, Bob and I still had children moving in and out of the house, and I was finally getting around to enrolling in some college classes. Up to the day Bob retired, I struggled to be a good corporate wife, though never really succeeding. Another ongoing struggle was trying to fill the role of perfect daughter for my mother. I never managed to fine-tune that, either. Instead of grieving for Daddy, I moved on to the things that were demanding my immediate attention and begging for my time. It was easier to bury my grief right then than try to deal with it.

At the time, I didn't think structured grieving was vital for me, because I have always been such a strong person. Daddy taught me to be strong. Strong physically, strong emotionally and, yes, strong headed. I turned out just like him — exactly as he had trained me.

When the Women's Liberation Movement first surfaced — the one during my lifetime — it was difficult for me to understand its mission. Daddy had convinced me from my early days to believe there was nothing I couldn't do if I set my mind to it. He taught me that all it took was a sense of fair play, adequate preparation, and a lot of hard work. He reared me for the real world by making me believe his theory of success — not as a woman's issue, but as a fact.

I know Mother didn't think much of him creating a female version of himself. She made that very clear by criticizing my every unladylike action. Believe me when I tell you that it added up to a lot of criticism.

Daddy was a unique person, as are we all, but he was just a little more so. It would not reflect accuracy to call him a minister. He believed in all things good and tried to practice what he preached, but he ministered as if only he knew the right way to do things — and as far as I knew, he was usually right. He was more like a minister of justice. He was not THE minister of justice, for as close as he ever came to politics was to read the local newspaper, see which candidates the editorial staff was endorsing, then go to the polls and vote for the other guy, figuring that one to be a deserving underdog.

If Daddy is helping me formulate these thoughts, and I am quite sure he is, he would want me to include one more part of this description. To this day, I frequently refer to myself as the daughter of a red-necked Irishman.

I was pretty old before I learned of such a thing as anger control. It never occurred to me that Daddy's way of handling life's little injustices might be a product of his own hard headedness — that his readiness to engage in fisticuffs at the drop of a bowler might not be the proper way to handle things. I only knew that he did what he thought was right. As a child, I was led to believe it was just his Irish blood boiling up, as it did from time to time. And I believed that for many years.

Daddy was without steady employment for a long time due to the hardships caused by the crash of the stock market and the lengthy depression that followed. President

Franklin Delano Roosevelt was creating wonderful solutions on our behalf, but relief from those hardships took a complicated and circuitous path to our front door. Building jobs were as scarce as the flow of money. By trade, Daddy was a carpenter and an iron worker, but not too proud to take any kind of job that would keep his family living in our modest home and away from the soup kitchens. At that time, he had five mouths to feed.

John, or Bud as he was called, my eldest brother, carried the weight of the world on his shoulders. He was a handsome, dark-haired, somber, studious, artistic, thoughtful and very responsible child. After he started to school, my parents recognized the dangers of him crossing 15th Street twice a day and found a little house to rent on the school side of the busy thoroughfare. Soon after the move, Mother told Daddy that Bud was even later coming home than before. Daddy walked up to the school to watch him and see what was causing his tardiness. To his dismay, Daddy watched Bud walk his young friends down to 15th Street, outstretch his arms to hold them back, and then when it was safe to cross, hurry them across the street. Bud stood and watched very carefully before making his way back across to return to his safe new home.

Fred was three years younger. This happy-go-lucky, red-haired, freckle-faced Irish lad loved to make people happy. He was fast-moving, witty, fun-loving and musically talented in both voice and piano. Fred knew no secrets. I am sure his teacher had a lengthy agenda to discuss with his parents when she asked if they would be coming to the parent-teacher conferences. Fred's reply was, "Probably will, if Dad can find a clean shirt to wear." His blue eyes danced when he added, "One that is both clean *and* ironed."

I was born the year that Fred started kindergarten. My mother let me know early on that my birth had not been planned, but Daddy always made me feel wanted. I guess Mother was too busy trying to keep hearth and home together to make me feel much of anything.

Dennis was born after I had completed high school and was engaged to be married the first time. Not married the first time — engaged the first time. I have only been married once. I only intend to be married once.

Several people asked me if it didn't embarrass me for my mother to be pregnant. It didn't embarrass me. Nor did I understand the question. Why should I be embarrassed? I didn't have anything to do with it. In fact, her pregnancy with Dennis and my eventual two pregnancies might have been the closest my mother and I ever managed to be.

Late one evening, Mother came down the stairs looking pretty frumpy, as if she had rolled out of bed and dressed without even running a comb through her hair. My fiancé couldn't think of an appropriate response when she abruptly asked him to leave. He nodded, turned to me and said, "I'll give you a call tomorrow," and left.

Mother always claimed she liked the young man, and I couldn't imagine her being that rude to him. I closed the door, turned the key, and before I could verbally fly into Mother, as I was prone to do, she cut me short, as she was very often prone to do, and she ordered, "Go get your daddy up; it's time to go to the hospital."

Oh!

Daddy was so proud of Dennis. When we brought him home from the hospital, Daddy would cradle him in his arms and walk him around and around the dining room table singing, "Oh, Denny Boy," in his Irish tenor voice.

Usually, Daddy's Irish brogue would surface just before his Irish temper flared. My earliest recollection of Daddy's boiling Irish blood took place before I started to school.

We had just arrived home from church, and the boys

and I were instructed to change into our play clothes.

My dresses were made from muslin sacks, which Daddy brought home from the feed store. I was growing so fast that it now took more than one sack for Mother to make my dresses. It was becoming more and more difficult to find two sacks with the same flowers printed on them. The only way I could tell which was my good dress was to feel it and determine if it had been ironed and was still fluffy. If it wasn't, it was fair game to be labeled as play clothes.

I stood before Mom while she tied the sash in the back of my dress. She asked Daddy, "Do you think we can spare enough money for Fred to take some hot dogs to his Sunday school picnic this afternoon?"

"How many are you talking about?" Daddy asked.

"We should probably send a whole pound, in case someone else shows up empty-handed," Mom replied. "If you don't think we can afford it, I can wrap up an oleo and sugar sandwich for him."

Daddy started to say something, then paused. The tension in his face broke into a smile, and Daddy winked at me and said, "No, we can manage."

When Daddy would first stand up, sometimes he moved like his own daddy. The carpenters and bricklayers in my family sometimes moved like they had to get warmed up first.

Daddy turned and said, "Want to go to the store with me, Pal?" He held out his hand, and I skipped up to place mine inside his. Daddy's hands were always scarred, rough and scaly, but they were always like a haven to my hands. When he would come home from work, he would take out his pocketknife to remove any splinters that had lodged in his hands, and he would send me scurrying to fetch the Mercurochrome, which he called "monkey blood."

I would have gone to the moon with Daddy if only

he'd asked me. I loved going places with him, but I had been taught that when he wanted me to go, it would be he who did the asking. I knew how to stand right in his line of vision and kind of twist my toe into the ground so that he had a hard time ignoring me. Not that he ever tried.

Daddy would sometimes forget who was walking with him, and I would have to add a little hop and a couple of running steps every so often to keep up. I only had to do this three or four times, then he would slow down or take smaller steps.

When Daddy and I took trips together, he would ask me about important things: had the boys allowed me to join in any of their games; if so, what games had we played; had I been to visit either of my grandmothers that week?

There were no little girls in our neighborhood, and I had no dolls of my own, so I would sometimes make my own paper dolls, cutting the models from the Sears Roebuck catalog and dressing them with my own crayon-fashioned designs.

We didn't turn at the corner where I thought we should, and I asked, "Daddy, aren't we going to Morty's Market?"

"Just thought we'd try a new store today," he replied.

I wondered if it had anything to do with Mom's parting remark, telling him that we couldn't get any more credit from Morty. I didn't ever remember buying any credit, nor did I remember Mom ever cooking any. Just as well. It probably tasted like Brussels sprouts anyway.

I was entering unfamiliar territory, so everything caught my attention. Daddy and I were still walking hand in hand as we walked past the carrots with their fluffy green topknots; past the plump red tomatoes, with their green stems still attached. We never bought stuff like this at the store, because we grew them in our own garden. Our garden was so big that we didn't have it in our backyard any more. We

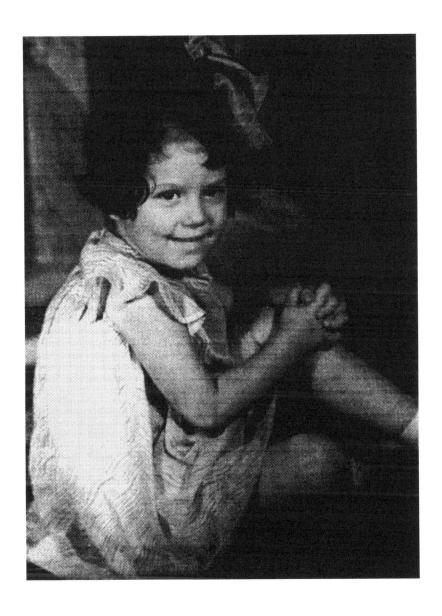

Ann Elizabeth Milholland, age 3

had it in somebody else's vacant lot about six blocks away. The boys had to work there. They had to hoe in the beginning and then pick the beans, tomatoes, corn and peas, but I didn't. I thought that was their punishment for not letting me tag along with them and their friends.

I kicked at the red sawdust on the floor that smelled like furniture wax, and we went on past the onions, potatoes and canned goods, right to the meat counter in the rear of the store.

I wondered how Daddy knew where to find it. He knew everything.

We stood looking over the contents of the glass case. I blew on the glass to see if I could draw pictures while I waited, but nothing happened. I reached out to touch the glass to see if it felt cold. It didn't feel as cold as the glass at Morty's store.

The butcher stepped up to his side of the counter and said, "What do you need?"

Daddy asked, "How much are you getting for hot dogs today?"

Maybe it was that soggy old cigar butt in the corner of the butcher's mouth that made him look like he'd put his smile on upside down that morning. He didn't even answer Daddy, but instead jerked his thumb toward a hand-printed sign hanging on a wire above his head. Since I couldn't read yet, I didn't have a clue until the butcher said, "You even got a dime on ya, buddy?"

"Oh, oh!" I thought. I wondered why he said that. He didn't know us. Was it the way we looked? Our clothes may not have been very fancy, but I knew it was important to Mom that we were always clean. I checked to see if my hands and face were still clean from going to church that morning. I looked at my hands and felt my face. They were still clean. I glanced at Daddy's, and his were, too.

James Joseph Milholland, probably looking toward the distant shores of Galway Bay, about which he often sang in his crystal tenor voice.

My eyes darted up to Daddy's face. He said, "Wrap me a pound of your freshest, plumpest hot dogs, please." I could see his face taking on his steely expression — the one where his left eyebrow would cock just a little higher than his right one. It meant that Daddy's Irish blood was beginning to simmer and could boil over at any time. This happened when people didn't do right by him.

I was only tall enough to see through the front glass and out the back glass, which the butcher had left ajar. I could see the wooden table with the meat cleaver stuck in the top of it. I heard the rumble of the big wooden roller as he pulled out a square of white paper that was slick on one side. He tore it off, then reached in the case and pulled out a string of wieners that were all still hanging together and only tied off every once in a while. He placed them on the paper, and it all went into the white enamel basket that hung on the bottom of the scale. It was hanging up so high that I had to back up to see it. That string must not have been enough, because he broke off two more and placed them up with the others.

"What else?" he asked.

"Nothing, thanks, that'll be it for today," Daddy replied.

I peered through the glass and heard the scales bounce as the butcher pulled the paper with the meat on it down to my level. He placed them on the chop block, and a gasp escaped from my throat as I watched him push the two extra wieners aside before wrapping the paper into a tight roll.

My oversized Sunday-go-to-meetin' hair bow was still securely nestled in my thick hair, but I felt it flop against my head as I turned to see if Daddy saw what I saw. His eyes were closing to a skinny little squint. That meant that he was thinking hard. I knew he had seen it, too.

I looked back in time to see the butcher pull a piece of

white paper tape off of a roller that looked as if it had a nasty, bristly black mustache, all gummed up with glue. He secured the package with the damp tape, pressed it down hard and rubbed it back and forth a couple of times. He took the black grease pencil from behind his ear and marked on the outside of the paper, then handed it across the counter to Daddy.

Neither of them said a word, which was not like Daddy at all, because he loved to visit with everyone. I would sometimes get the heebie-jeebies behind my knees, waiting for him to finish talking. The few times I complained about them, Daddy explained that those were growin' pains. But I think they were talkin' pains.

I knew for a fact that all was not right with the world by the length of Daddy's steps.

I looked at Daddy's grip on the white package. His hand was big enough to almost go clear around it, and his knuckles were white. I was running as fast as my short little legs could pump, barely able to keep up as we forged our way to the front of the store. Daddy placed the package in the basket of the scales that hung up over the carrots, onions and potatoes.

This must not have been my first big adventure with Daddy, because when we retraced our steps to the meat department at the same rate of speed we had left it, I instinctively stepped behind some heavy wooden shelving to watch what was coming next.

Daddy walked back to his former position in front of the meat counter, leaned back, stuck his left hand out in front of him about shoulder-high for counterbalance. I watched as he cocked his right hand behind his ear in what appeared to be a perfect baseball windup, and let that package fly with a powerhouse delivery right to the strike zone.

The missile found a solid hit on the right ear of the

unsuspecting butcher, making a vicious smacking noise at the moment of impact. The tape hadn't had time to dry yet, and the explosion sent that string of hot dogs straight up in the air, coming to rest on the wire that held the meat prices along with some little pie-shaped red flags. The hot dogs swung back and forth like a string of fat, ugly, wiggly worms.

I peeked around the opposite end of my wooden shelves, which allowed me clear vision of what was going on behind the meat counter. I saw the butcher stagger a step or two. He blinked his eyes several times and reached to steady himself on his chop block. He adjusted his glasses, then his little white paper hat, and I watched him slide his hand over the handle of the meat cleaver and tighten his grip.

He started around my end of the meat counter, and I hollered, "Here he comes, Daddy."

Daddy must have already scouted his options, for he backed up to a shelf of canned goods, reached behind him, wrapped his hand around a great big can of something, all without ever taking his eyes off the butcher. He brought the can around in front of him, held it as if it was ready to wind up behind his right ear, too, and calmly asked the butcher, "Do you want some more?"

I could tell the butcher gave it some thought, but he must have decided he didn't. He stared at Daddy for what seemed like a week or 10 days before he eased back behind the counter again.

I joined Daddy as we stepped up to our side of the counter again, just as if it was our first trip up to bat — except this time Daddy wasn't smiling. He was still holding the big can and tossing it up in the air just enough to make the label turn around a little more each time it landed in his hand. He gave the butcher one more lengthy opportunity to view his steely blue eyes; then he didn't *ask* him this time, he *told* him. "Wrap up a *full* pound of hot dogs and we'll be on our way."

He did and we were.

Going places with Daddy was kind of like going through life with the Lone Ranger. We administered justice wherever we went. Daddy always made sure I understood exactly what precipitated his behavior when we encountered someone doing wrong. Once we were outside of the store, Daddy pulled me up close to the building, stooped down so we were at the same eye level and asked me, "Do you understand what went on in there?" I replied that I did. He wanted to make sure I knew that man had tried to cheat us. Daddy's earnest little talks with me were never like apologies — they were only explanations.

I never knew when we set out from home whether or not there would be the righting of a wrong before we returned, but I never stayed home because of them. I went to as many places with Daddy as I was invited. Sometimes Mom would interfere and not allow me to go, for whatever reason, but this made her the bad guy, never him.

chapter two

MY EYELIDS WERE SHOWING no signs of getting heavy. The drone of the airplane engines should have helped me entertain thoughts of sleep. Instead, I watched the passengers pacing up and down the aisles, as if they knew something I didn't know and were passing the knowledge on to others as they stopped to talk in what they considered to be a whisper.

I pulled my backpack up from between my feet and took out the small notebook I had brought along to use for my genealogical research on the O'Hagerty branch of my family tree.

One of my recent developments had been a good sign. My interest in genealogy had begun to yawn, then twist into a stretch and was now scratching its way back into my consciousness. It had been at rest for more than 20 years.

I scanned the notes I had copied from my genealogy albums. I knew that my great-grandfather, Patrick Joseph, was born to Patrick and Mary Sheridan O'Hagerty on January 6, 1847, during the potato famine. He was the second of ten children, and the family sailed for America in 1855. That is all I know about my O'Hagertys, except that they dropped the "O" from their name when they left Ireland.

I admired all of the emigrants just for the effort they had expended for survival. I knew I was totally incapable of understanding what they must have endured. How forbidding it must have been to take that first step on board a ship that had been labeled a "death ship" because so many would die before the end of their journey. Then be transported to a foreign country where you must learn to live anew in an unknown culture. How empty they must have felt leaving behind their loved ones, relationships, familiar surroundings and lifelong experiences.

Emptiness can sometimes be replaced by hope, but you seldom experience an even trade. The scales in your life frequently remain a little out of balance. This is probably why so many Irish ballads deal with how much the writers miss their beloved Ireland and how they struggle to deal with their yearnings to return to their homeland.

It was hard to face the realization that I had stopped caring whether I lived or died and had actually lost hope. My children had truly been the forces that kept me going.

My son lives near me and my daughter is a nine-hour drive away. She and her husband have my only grandchild. I love them individually and collectively, but even with their support, I occasionally continue to lose my direction.

The smaller my world becomes, the more important each member of my dwindling family becomes. But this is only when I am thinking rationally. Other times I want to throw in the towel and quit trying.

Back when I was so focused on researching my families, the more I knew about family members, the more I wanted to know. Not only their names, but also what their lives were like, where they lived, how they happened to be living there, how they earned their daily bread. I had an insatiable appetite for more information.

There is no place I would rather be when I am away from home than in Ireland. I agreed to the magnificent area of Connemara this time because I decided, from all I had read that this was where I might find the peace and serenity I was desperately seeking.

Intellectually, I knew that everything I had been reading was being filtered through my own needs, but deep in my heart I felt that the beauty of God's earthly handiwork might help me at least mend a portion of my injured soul. My need to be in the northwest part of Ireland more than any other place in the world just felt so right. In my family tree, the biggest limbs still missing belonged to my paternal grandparents; my grandmother was a Hagerty, and my grandfather was a Milholland.

James and Charles left Ireland as Mulhollands. When they reached America, their paths split. James changed the "u" to an "i," and we became Milhollands.

I told Dennis that, on this trip to Ireland, we should concentrate on the O'Hagertys and see if we could find any traces of them. We know a whole lot about Patrick's wife and her family, but the O'Hagertys who came from around Clifden and County Mayo remained a mystery. I must not have been at my station under the dining room table on the Sunday the family discussed them — or they were never discussed.

The seed of my interest in ancestors was planted at my paternal grandparents' home, when I was a very small child. On a typical Sunday afternoon, I would concentrate on the slim time slot between the end of dinner and the moment the womenfolks would start to clean up after the meal.

Standing like a hunting dog on point, with nothing moving but my eyeballs, I would watch to see if anyone was watching me watch them. If not, I would stretch up high on my tippy toes, grab a double handful of black olives, and slip under the table.

My grandmother's Sunday white tablecloth was large enough to fall down on all four sides, far enough to supply the privacy I needed to remain unnoticed.

As I leaned against a table leg, I began to line up naked olive pits like fallen soldiers on the trestle of the table. To clutch them in my fist would make my hand all damp and puckered. I had to remember to take my regiment of defeated warriors with me when I came out of hiding.

Black olives were only one of the many good things about having dinner at my grandparents' house on Sundays. I loved playing with my cousins, but I preferred listening to stories even more. I think everyone talking about hard times was part of it, too. But I was not sure how. I wasn't quite sure what hard times meant but, whatever it was, we sure enjoyed a lot of good dinners in the big white house where Maw and Granddaddy lived.

Three of my cousins lived next door, so we could explore the wilderness of the grape arbor and feast in our hideout anytime. There was always the need of a meeting in the clubhouse we had built, but we could do these things when we visited during the week. The rest of the cousins, who eventually totaled 14, were lucky enough to live within a few miles of each other. That also encouraged as many as possible to come together on Sundays to be a family unit.

I lined up the last of my olive pits and pulled my dress down over my legs to make sure that my underpants didn't show. This was just in case someone should look under the tablecloth — you know, if I happened to explode with a laugh, a sneeze, or a cough.

I wished they would get started.

Do you suppose the reason my brothers would not share their friends with me was because I was never the last one to be selected when the guys chose up sides? I could run with the fastest of them and drop-kick a football almost as far as the best of them.

I did a lot of their dirty work for them, trying to be a part of the gang; I helped catch garter snakes for the boys to place inside their chewing gum boxes so they could politely offer gum to the girls at school. Once the boys took up a collection and offered me four pennies to chase Elmer home. They really, really didn't want Elmer tagging after them. I held out for five pennies, and they paid my asking price. All I had to do was chase him down the hill while dangling a dead mouse by its tail. I knew that only Elmer was afraid of the mouse, because the other boys had found it for me. They knew that if we got caught, the punishment would be a lot less severe on me than on any of them. I did everything they asked me to do. But they still didn't want me hanging around them.

On the occasions I was allowed to play with them, I was careful to tuck the hem of my dress into the elastic in the legs of my underpants. It never stayed very long, so they already knew what my underpants looked like. I don't know why this was such a big deal with my mother, anyway.

If God gave me a mother to see if she could make a lady out of me, He must be pretty disappointed with both of us.

I wrapped my dress tightly around my legs and hugged them. I placed my head on my knees and listened to the adults finally settle down to talk. They were scattered all around the dining room like buckshot. Two sat in the facing rocking chairs in the bay window. I could hear someone readjusting the metal bar on the back of the Morris chair that sat under the picture frame with the flowers designed from the hair of women in our family — eeew! The rest of the folks sat in straight-back chairs that matched the dining table. Thank goodness they had pushed them back against the walls or I would have had their stinky feet under the table with me. When this did happen, someone always took their shoes off.

It was hard to believe that despite all those people there, only one conversation was going at a time. I supposed that when you learned to do that without being told, it meant you were a grown-up.

I didn't recognize the voice that suggested Horace Greeley might be today's topic. They launched right into the beginning, which started, "Old Horace, the cousin, not the brother." I was hoping someone would ask who "Horace the cousin" was so I could mentally perch him up on the correct limb of the family tree, like one more stuffed bird.

Someone was bound to tell, even if everyone already knew. My relatives have always been very thorough story-tellers. As far as I know, not one person ever made an ounce of difference by saying they had already heard a story before. I think it must have been because everyone in our family considered our family to be so much more interesting than anyone else's and our stories well worth repeating over — and over — and over again.

Uncle Winfield was Daddy's favorite storyteller. The stories he told were so exciting. I heard Daddy tell the story about Uncle Winfield's brother, Ezra, who was a soldier during the Civil War. He was captured and eventually escaped from Libby Prison. Ezra only traveled at night to avoid getting caught. He slept in barns or in overgrown fields during the day. He ate nothing but the fruit that had fallen from the trees. I wondered if his stomach ached from eating too many apples, like mine did sometimes. I felt the sores on his feet from walking across four states. They must have felt like the blisters I got on my heels from my new school oxfords each fall. He hid from all of his enemies and all the people chasing him. He traveled nearly two thousand miles on foot to his home up north. When he arrived home, he found that the war ended the same day he escaped.

I would hide under the table to hear Daddy tell stories

like this again and again. And they would take hours to tell. His versions were so detailed, and I was right there with him every step of the way with my heart racing, my stomach growling and my feet hurting.

A portion of Uncle Winfield's own colorful life was spent as a Texas Ranger in Comanche County. One of the Rangers' duties was to ride into nearby towns, run the bad guys out or lock them up, and mend quarrels between neighbors. They did this because it was easier for outsiders to straighten things up and then take all of the hard feelings away with them when they left.

During my early years, children were governed by the "seen, but not heard" doctrine. In my mind, if they couldn't see me or hear me, I was twice as apt to stay out of trouble. At the time, I thought I was hiding under the table to delay my own bedtime, but, really, I was hiding under there because that's the way Daddy had done it to delay his bedtime. How long I could remain hidden depended on my age. The smaller I was, the sooner I would emerge and crawl into Daddy's lap to be lulled to sleep by the rhythm of his voice.

If the stories were not about family history, they were usually about what happened on the job sites that week. The work stories sent me high-tailing to join my cousins and see what kind of mischief they were creating.

I dearly loved hearing stories about the people listed on the framed floral registry that hung in my grandparents' entryway. There were beautiful flowers drawn on it, along with a boat on an ocean that read "The Voyage of Life," and birds with ribbons in their mouths, and a clock that revealed "The Eleventh Hour." I didn't like that clock running out, nor did I like the tiny little drawing that looked like a sunset showing "The End of Time." But I did like the morning glories and the rest of the drawing, which was by an artist who used a pen and black ink to draw the registry and then signed his name, Edgar Wilson.

I wish I could draw like that.

Family legend has it that it was on Harriet Gettys' family farm in Pennsylvania that the Battle of Gettysburg was fought. I have since tried to document the connection, but was told by a docent at the Gettysburg Historical Society that, back then, the name Gettys was about as common as the name Smith is today. I have not given up hope of determining the truth one way or the other someday.

The registry said my daddy's paternal grandmother, Caroline, was one of the 15 children born to Harriet Gettys Daniel and Henry Daniel. Uncle Winfield Daniel was the baby of that family. I had no trouble placing any of them on the proper limb of that tree because I could see it.

When our three O'Donald brothers sailed from Ireland, the captain of their ship told them all the Irish names sounded alike, so he dropped the "O" from their name and called them Donald. Charles O'Donald could neither read nor write, and when saying his name with his Irish brogue, people understood him to say either "Donnal" or "Dannel." By the time his lawyer wrote his will, he signed with an "X" under Dannel. Generations that followed continued to go by Dannel, eventually switching the spelling to Daniel, but regardless of the spelling, those in my family continued to pronounce it "Dannel."

On this particular Sunday, someone else decided that my daddy's maternal grandmother, Martha Greeley, would also be "the person of the day," along with Horace Greeley. Martha had a brother named Horace Greeley, but he was not the one who was famous for telling young men to go West. That was Horace, the cousin. The storyteller was careful to make that distinction.

Everyone contributing to this topic talked as if they already knew about Horace, the cousin, but like I said, that didn't keep the stories from being told again. This was lucky for me, for even if I hadn't been in hiding, my brothers and I were not allowed to interrupt adults while they were talking. Not even with questions. Not even with questions about the subject that was being discussed. Maybe that's another reason they were all so thorough — and repetitive.

In *Yourself and the Neighbours*, written in 1914, Seamus MacManus wrote, "They were the old, old tales that had come down to you ripened and sweetened like your pipe, with the ages — barring that the years of the tales were as the days of the pipe. And men and women were like little children listening even for the thousandth time, to the same tale; and could go without food or drink for fondness of hearing you tell them."

Personally, I preferred food and drink with my stories, and I didn't start tiring of Daddy's stories until about my fortieth year of age or the fortieth time to hear the same story — whichever came first. Right now, I would love to hear Daddy tell me another story, and it wouldn't matter how many times I had heard it.

Whoever was talking at the moment said "Horace Greeley, the cousin, was the founding editor of the *New York Tribune*, one of the first penny daily newspapers." But then added, "which was published weekly."

I remember wondering how you could have a daily newspaper that was published weekly. Anyway, his paper claimed over a million readers throughout the United States and the western territories, and our family was pretty darned proud of old Horace. Horace sounded important, even to me, but someone older than I should have asked about that daily/weekly thing.

As nearly as I could tell, Martha Greeley's father, Absalom, and Horace were first cousins.

The literal translation of (Grele) Greeley, was "grey meadow." I love the serenity of a meadow, even a grey one.

My Greeleys list Andrew Greeley (or Grelie) as the ancestor who came to America from England sometime before 1640. He settled in what is now known as Salisbury, Massachusetts. My direct line from the first Andrew filtered down through Philip, Jonathan, another Jonathan, Aaron, John, and finally my great-great-grandfather, Absalom.

Absalom and his wife, Millicent Roblyn, a first cousin to the prime minister of Manitoba, were both born and eventually married in Canada. The first of their 10 children was Martha, my great-grandmother.

Martha, the beautiful pride and joy of her doting parents, was just beginning to broaden her world by learning to walk and was still very unstable on her feet. Her wobbly antics provided many delights for her mamma and papa. One day, as she was weaving around the parlor, she lost her balance and clutched the nearest thing to her. Unfortunately it was the cloth covering the parlor table, which came crashing down with Martha, along with the pot of steaming, freshly brewed tea. The scalding liquid splashed over her, resulting in severe burns over a great portion of her tiny little body.

Absalom and Millicent's firstborn lay for days struggling to survive. After her recovery, she spent the rest of her days reaching deep within herself for the courage to deal with her disfigurement. She suffered the loss of an eye, along with unsightly scars on her face, neck, chest, and shoulder.

Our only photograph of Martha shows her dress beginning high up under her chin, trimmed out in beautiful lace, bedecked with a brooch, designed specifically for maximum coverage of her scars.

Martha's impaired physical beauty did not keep her from blooming into a pleasant young lady.

Martha (Greeley) Hagerty

She could barely contain her excitement when her father, a member of Canadian Provincial Parliament, informed her that the Prince of Wales would be coming to Canada for an official visit. As the eldest unmarried daughter, Martha was eligible to accompany her parents to the ball being held to honor the prince.

Martha's mother summoned their dressmaker to initiate the preliminary measures for making ball gowns. Special materials and trimmings had to be ordered.

Martha's excitement was short-lived, however. She learned that the list of strict rules of protocol had been posted, then distributed. This particular event called for bare shoulders of all young ladies in attendance.

The silk shawl with the satin embroidery and the hand-carved ivory fan Martha's father ordered from India to assist in covering her scars were destined to become only family heirlooms, and nothing more, for it was Martha's decision that she would not attend. Her younger sisters did not qualify to take her place, so her parents attended the ball alone.

In her twentieth year, Martha's parents moved her into the nearby town of Picton to attend finishing school. She hated leaving her country home, for she loved the farm, the dairy and the cheese factory. More than those reasons, she hated being separated from her sisters and brothers.

Out of loneliness, Martha began writing detailed accounts of her thoughts and feelings, as well as composing poetry in her journal. Her journal was her dearest friend. During the course of her writing, she captured the attention of the nosy lady who ran the school. When pressed, Martha stood firm and refused to allow her to read the diary, even though it appeared pretty certain that the intruder with the unpleasant disposition had already done so.

In her diary, Martha related how this woman reported her "outrageous diary" to her mother out of spite for not handing it over. Millicent was not upset about her daughter's diary, nor did she ask to see it. As a matter of privacy, Martha found a better place to hide it, and for added security chose to stop writing rather than risk anyone else reading her private thoughts.

I was an adult when I read Martha's journal, but it still made me feel somewhat intrusive and a trifle uncomfortable. But those feelings were quickly overridden by my feelings of gratitude.

On March 22, 1872, Martha resumed writing.

"It is almost five years since I have written a word in this journal and there have been many changes since then. Pa was elected member for the Legislature of Ontario, two years after he was appointed Sheriff of the county. Now he is the Lord knows where — his enemies have tried for years to ruin him — they have succeeded at last and he was obliged to leave the country and everything we have will be sold (at auction) tomorrow."

Absalom's problems were seldom mentioned and never detailed by Martha in her journal. They were only referred to as "the trouble" or "Papa's troubles."

From under the dining room table, I learned that Great-great-grandfather Absalom Greeley was accused of being an English sympathizer during Canada's bid for independence. He was forced to flee Canada in the middle of the night, leaving Millicent and the children behind to dispatch the domestics, the governess, the dairy and farm workers; then dispose of their possessions and land holdings, and join him in Minnesota.

Martha's greatest sacrifice was leaving behind her beloved rosewood piano, on which she had been giving lessons to her two younger sisters. She wrote, "When her papa purchased it, the price of the piano had been $500, but we had only had to pay $425 for it." It truly was her treasure.

Martha wrote, "Mr. Norman bid off the wine glasses and decanters for himself and made Ma a present of them. On Friday I went to Picton with Jonathan to get some boots for the children, cloth for Horace, Nathan and Appa's clothes; and lawn (material) for traveling suits for the rest of us."

Their move to Minnesota drastically altered their standard of living and their life style, eventually cutting into the richness of their family as a whole. No explanation was given why they only received the price of one cow, or $30, from the results of the sale of all their holdings.

They all moved and lived together in the United States. Martha continued to write, saying that they arrived in Minnesota with only about $100 in their pockets.

Closing that chapter of her life, her next entry was not until April 17, 1873.

"It is over a year since I have written in this book and I scarcely know where to begin or what to write first. We are living in the City of Faribault, Rice County, in the State of Minnesota."

In July most of the family was stricken with typhoid. The neighbors were very kind to them, and Martha mentioned that the minister brought them peaches every week. After they recovered their good health, they tried to keep boarders. They only had two, who paid $8.00 per week plus 75 cents per day for washing. She didn't explain whether that cost was for washing their bodies or their clothing.

Martha related that Pa was doing very well with his new skill of electroplating. His office and workplace were in one part of the house, while they lived in the remainder.

Eliza learned dressmaking and was serving with Mrs. Crandell for 50 cents per day, trying to pay for a sewing machine.

Horace was working in Gates' Feed Store, receiving $15 per month.

Patrick Joseph Hagerty

Nathan started to school, but Flora didn't, because they could not dress her decently and still buy the books she needed.

In December 1875 most of Martha's family moved to Kansas City, Missouri, leaving her behind. She did not reveal the reason for her abandonment.

At the age of 30, she was baptized and married to Patrick Joseph Hagerty on the same day, January 22, 1876.

"I wrote to tell my family, in hopes that they would answer, even if it was just to give me a scolding, but instead, they were very, very angry. My sisters vowed never to speak to me again."

This is the portion of her diary that still lights a fire inside of me, her great-granddaughter. I would love to know if her family disowned Martha because they still needed her monetary contribution toward the well-being of the family, or because her new husband was poor. It may also have been because of the couple's new church. Patrick had been a member of the Anglican Church of England and Martha was Episcopalian. Both were austere and ritualistic in their churches before joining the Catholic Church. She only stated in her diary that she "was baptized and married on the same day."

Down deep in my heart, I hope Martha wasn't disowned because Patrick was Irish, because at this point, I still have a tiny little bit of room in my heart to forgive them for treating their daughter as they did.

"When we were in Canada rich and prosperous," Martha wrote, "we went in the best society of course it was different after we came here and each one had to earn our own living. The first thing I did was to get the fever and after I got over that everything was changed. I was an 'Old Maid' and an old shoe to be kicked about by some of the more stylish members of the family. After I began teaching I was

'Old French Irish.' Of course a person teaching in the country is not in the most aristocratic place in the world, but strange to say, the money is just as acceptable as if it was earned in town. All that I ever earned they got at home with the exception of a calico dress each (school) term and a pair of boots each year."

In November 1876, the first Hagerty daughter was born; in 1878 the second daughter; in 1880, the third daughter.

Martha's last entry in the diary was March 20, 1880, stating, "They have been writing for me and my family to go and live where they are and I suppose we will before long."

But the rift never mended.

My grandmother was the third Hagerty daughter mentioned in Martha's diary. She was named Margaret Ann, and it was to honor her that her second name was given to me. When she grew big enough, she hired out as a domestic to contribute to her family's livelihood.

Listening from under the table, I had to wipe my eyes and my nose with the tail of my dress when I learned that she would walk by her grandparents' beautiful home with holes in her shoes and not wearing a proper coat. Sometimes she was almost too tired or too hungry to finish the long walk home, but her grandparents would watch her pass by and never speak a word to her. Nor did they offer to share any of their comforts with her or the rest of the Hagerty family.

As I read Martha's diary, it was easy for me to identify with her and assume her bitterness as my own, for she appeared to be such a lonely woman struggling with the need to show her worth to anyone who would notice.

There were few problems collecting information about the Greeleys, but I wanted to know more about the O'Hagertys — however little it might be. I know the year they came to America and the year Patrick was born. I know that they lived in and near the town of Clifden and also in County Mayo. When Patrick was eight years of age, they dropped the "O" from in front of their name and sailed for America. I also know that they were poor. How can any of these facts be a big enough threat to fracture a family, separating out one of their own children?

Why didn't these people understand that your family is the most important thing in your life?

I need to find my connection to my O'Hagertys in Ireland. I need to find my family ties. I need to find my Irish family.

chapter three

I HAVE BEEN PLODDING through the murky depths of widowhood hand-in-hand with my grief. Sometimes I am a leader and sometimes I am a follower. Even when I am a leader, I don't feel as if I am in control of anything. I have at least been able to surface, cleanse myself from much of the heaviness that has been stifling my heart. Why have I been able to work through most of this for my husband, who died only eight months ago, but not for my daddy, who died 15 years ago? Is my need for finding my Irish roots or any tie to Ireland becoming my way of dealing with Daddy?

I was told by a trusted friend, who is also a grief counselor, that I should not make any major decisions or expect to successfully complete my healing process until I have experienced every emotion, every season, every holiday, every birthday and every anniversary without my husband.

I have already made it past all of the holidays between January and the end of August, as well as the tail end of winter, spring and summer. I have experienced and dealt with the fact that I would never share another wedding anniversary with my husband, except to place flowers on his grave. I am about to experience the beginning of the autumn season.

I stepped off the airplane onto Irish soil the morning of my birthday. I wasn't sure which one, for what difference did it make? Physically, I was exhausted. Emotionally,

I felt as if I needed to wrap myself in a cocoon so securely that no further injuries could possibly find me — even if my retreat was only for a short period of time. I was searching for a warmth found in some kind of protective covering that would hide me from the dings and bruises that kept battering my heart.

I switched over to a physical struggle in claiming my luggage and getting it up on the cart. I looked for the shortest line through customs, but my experience is that the shortest line usually takes the longest to work through, so I picked the closest. I answered the customary three questions and emerged through the double doors to find Dennis standing in the front of the receiving line.

He threw me a big grin along with his open arms. I was so relieved to hug someone who would take over my life for a while.

"Welcome to Dublin, Sis. And happy birthday!"

"Thanks, little bro."

"God, I hope you're not as weary as you look."

"Count on it. I need a bed in the worst way."

"You can't do bed just yet. I know you have had at least one wake-up breakfast on the plane, but I have a special birthday treat all prepared for you."

One of his great hobbies is chef-type cooking, but I was consumed with overwhelming fatigue and I was relieved to find that my birthday breakfast consisted of a chocolate (my favorite) Marge Simpson (not my favorite) birthday cake to go with my fourth cup of coffee.

I didn't even pull back the duvet before I crashed in the middle of his bed. I was finally able to shut down my senses for an hour, while Dennis added his essentials to my belongings already in the car. In addition to his clothing, he packed up his computer, coffeepot, first aid kit, a torch (what I call a flashlight) in case of power outage, along with assorted other things he thought we might need in the next month. He got me to an upright position in the car and off we went to Galway.

It takes the same amount of time to drive across the middle of Ireland — from Dublin to Galway — as it takes to drive across the middle of the state of Missouri — from Kansas City to St. Louis. Three hours later we arrived and found our townhouse in Salthill, which stands between downtown Galway and the promenade of Galway Bay.

Our landlord also owned a bakery and was waiting for us with a loaf of fresh brown bread and a jar of homemade strawberry jam. This is so typical of the Irish. When we rented a holiday house on the southeast coast a couple of years before, we were greeted with fresh flowers, a bottle of wine, and about an hour visit from our landlady.

We took off in search of a good restaurant to have lunch before stocking the larder. I ran out of gas all at once and asked if Dennis would shop for groceries while I dealt with some serious jet lag. He had no problem with this.

The glass of Guinness I had with my seafood chowder at Brusker Brown's pub greatly facilitated my collapse, and what I thought would be just a nap lasted straight through till morning. I took care of my lost night of sleep and my lost six hours all in one shot.

What a bright new day.

"Good morning, sunshine." Dennis laughed as he observed my over-sized sleep shirt, my bare feet, and my permanently pressed hair pointing 12 different directions.

"Good morning, sir." I stretched my arms over my head, then began to scratch the back of my opposite shoulder adding to my scraggly appearance.

"If you aren't a sight to behold."

"Hush," I cautioned him with my fist.

"I went to the market last evening while you caught up on your beauty sleep. I think your beauty sleep may be a task in progress, but I won't have to look at you all day. I got a call from one of the magazines I contribute to on a regular basis and they want me to submit a follow-up article to one of my previous articles. I will probably be busy most of today and maybe part of tomorrow."

"No problem." Just knowing he was close if I needed him was a great comfort and would help me spread my wings a little.

I showered, tried to make myself a little more presentable, grabbed some toast and coffee, and struck out on my own.

I spent the morning walking, exploring, feeding the swans on the river, and trying to get my bearings in a town full of narrow, circular streets. I figured I had better do it while the sun was shining, even though I am unable to navigate on this side of the globe the same as I do on the other side.

I stopped at the Tourist Office and sorted through all kinds of options. I found a brochure about a famine village in Connemara called Lettercraff. A lady behind one of the many smiling faces who stood ready to help with anything I needed was wearing a name tag that told me her name was Margaret. Margaret located a guide, named Edward, who agreed to take me to Lettercraff early the next day.

I knew that Dennis would not be joining me, but I booked Edward anyway.

I thanked Margaret and started to leave but, instead, turned and asked, "Where is Lettercraff located?"

"It is north and west of Galway in a region called Connemara."

"Will we be close to Clifden?"

"No, Lettercraff is located about halfway between

Galway and Clifden," she told me. "Do you want to go to Clifden?"

"Yes, eventually. I am on one of those mad genealogical searches."

"Do you have a car?" she asked.

"We rented one for the drive down, but my brother turned it back into the agency last night."

Margaret reached under the counter and handed me a bus schedule. She said, "Here, you might need this."

"Thank you."

I sat down on a park bench, ate a sandwich, leaned back with my face to the sun, closed my eyes, and tried to remember all I had read about Connemara.

It is the region to which Oliver Cromwell banished Catholic landowners during the mid-1600s, in the belief or hope that the land northwest of Galway was too poor and rocky for them to grow enough crops to survive. He was nearly correct, for even today in spite of all of its beauty it is nearly impossible to survive in this area if you live only from the land.

In 1845, the potato famine hit the western portion of the country, and the land was not to be fruitful again until the 1849 harvest. The blight not only stripped these people of their nutrition and livelihood, but it claimed huge numbers of lives.

Landlords began to suffer from their losses and felt justified in raising the rent in an effort to help balance out their own loss of revenue. The rent rose so high that the tenants could no longer pay and when they were evicted had nowhere to go.

Whole families were seen walking toward either Galway or Clifden, only to find the efforts for public assistance and the public works projects completely overwhelmed. These hardships eventually broke the spirit of these people and they began to die. Emigration equaled the numbers of the dying.

Those who remained in Ireland proved to be hardy people who cared about and looked after each other. They survived the harshness of the land and became even more proud of their Irish heritage.

I sat up to relieve the pressure on my lower back, but had a hard time opening my eyes. I was amazed at the courage of the famine survivors, showing an inner strength that reflected qualities that made me proud to be a part of them. Then, I thought, *"If I am proud to be a part of them, why can't I be more like them?"*

I may never be able to locate the exact place from where my O'Hagerty roots had been transplanted, but I felt I was about to experience a visit to their kind of village — maybe even their village. The next day, I would visit Lettercraff.

My first response to another bright new day was to identify the smell of a peat fire burning nearby. I rolled over, glanced at the clock, and inhaled deeply. I so welcomed the ability to sleep with the open windows and no screens. This was what I called the end of summer, and I snuggled deeper under the sheet and feather duvet. At home, my house would still be closed up tight with my laboring air-conditioner protecting me.

There is no other aroma on earth like burning peat — for it is earth. Burning a piece of sod that is thousands of years old, perhaps dug from an area where my forebears had lived, or perhaps walked, truly put me in tune with Mother Earth and Mother Ireland. It is like inhaling a piece of your ancestry into your lungs.

I reluctantly tested the temperature by sticking one foot out from under the covers, jumped out of bed, ran to the bathroom to turn on the heater, then crawled back in bed and waited for warmth to return to my body. I still missed snuggling.

My guide, Edward, steered me away from the middle and over to the side of the gate, opposite the lock. "Always put your weight on the hinge-bearing side of a gate," he warned. "It is sturdier." He helped me over first.

A soon-to-be-sheared ewe, sporting identifying red and blue paint sprays on her back, broke away from her flock and fell in step ahead of us, as if she had been selected to serve as our leader. Like sheep, we followed.

As we worked our way up the mountain, I asked Edward if he was a believer of ancient Irish mythology. He turned to look at me, as if I was testing his sincerity. "Some of it is believable to me, but not all of it," he admitted.

"Same with me. I can't quite manage with the world of the little ones who live under the ground."

He said no more.

"Weren't the children of one of the kings turned into animals?"

Still no answer.

I tried once more. "And didn't they live in animal bodies for eight or nine hundred years, while still retaining their human minds?"

His silence told me that he didn't want to continue this conversation, so I let my own thoughts skim the remainder of the legend. The Christians came to Ireland and turned them back into people. They were old and haggard, but retained the power to both console and heal.

I stooped to pick a bristly branch of heather and wondered if the struggle to detach it was perhaps due to some little person underneath hanging on to the flower on her hat.

These little hat-wearers still supposedly connect humans to animals today and help us communicate with our ancient brothers and sisters of the animal world.

This might be why there are such healing powers taking place in hospitals and nursing homes today that use pets to calm the patients and sometimes even revive in them a new zest for life.

More than once I have looked deep into the eyes of my dog and could read his mind; more to the point, I could see him reading mine. I may be missing something by closing my mind to these little underground dwellers.

We continued to climb, getting closer to the first big pile of rocks. The gentle breeze became a light wind gaining in intensity and kicking up a gusty sense of mystique. I walked through an invisible veil that made my previous chatter so inane that I was embarrassed for having violated what was becoming an obvious demand for reverence.

We had arrived at the ruins of Lettercraff.

What looked like random piles of rock from the downhill side soon became well-formed rectangles, some as high as waist level, some a little taller. Many of the doorway openings were still intact. Though he could have easily stepped over a low spot in the wall, I watched Edward show his respect by walking through one of the door openings, as if coming to pay a visit.

After he entered, he turned to me and broke the silence. "Families with nothing left to eat and no place to turn took their last look at the light of day, went inside of their windowless cottages, barricaded their doors and, with their last shred of dignity, surrendered."

Breaking quite a long pause, I collected my thoughts and fought back tears. I asked, "Why were their cottages windowless?"

Edward replied barely above the whisper I had used,

The remains of a famine village called Lettercraff, located in the region of Connemara, Ireland. The families oftentimes took their thatch with them to protect them wherever they had to sleep.

saying, "These houses had no windows because the people who lived here were unable to pay the extra taxes. At that time, there was a 'window tax' imposed on them. A window was a luxury that none here could afford. These peasants paid their taxes to the farmers, the farmers in turn paid taxes to the squire, and the squire turned over the money to the landlord, so there were plenty of observers to oversee and tax any luxuries these people might try to enjoy."

As my mind continued to deal with the dreariness of daily living for these people, I withdrew from Edward — from the present — wondering if my Patrick O'Hagerty and his family had lived in a village similar to this. I walked to another site, unsuccessfully trying to blink back tears as I reflected on the plight of these poor people.

I assumed that the reason these foundations were only as tall as they were, was because the builders had stacked rocks as high as they could, then used thatch from there on up to enclose their homes.

The largest foundation we found was around 14 feet by 24 feet and must have housed one of the larger families. I tried to envision families with seven or eight children, all probably sleeping on beds of hay. It was still hard for me to see how they could physically arrange their bodies to exist in such a limited space.

Unlike the many stone fences throughout this area, which are designed to leave sufficient spaces to enable the gusty winds to go through them, these rock walls were much tighter and thicker to provide needed insulation.

Some of the cottages were attached by a single row of stacked rocks forming a fence. Outside of these common areas you could see the remains of gardens, which were still green as if awaiting someone to return and tend to them. Yet, the sheep were avoiding this lush green grass to nibble around the harshness of fading heather and other greenery that was succumbing to the onset of winter.

Edward and I walked in separate directions. After my vision cleared, we came together again in the middle of someone's garden and looked at the stones placed just around the edge, delineating ownership or perhaps some other type of boundary. Were they also taxed by the size of their gardens?

I stood looking at the uneven surfaces in the garden as Edward explained, "These ridges were how they planted their potatoes. Planting on the side of this hill made it self-draining. Of course, the English had their name for these ridges. They called them 'lazy beds.' They claimed the Irish were lazy people. Rather than digging drills for potatoes, which was the normal way of doing things, the Irish came up with this way of building ridges, and the English claimed it was a lazy way of doing their work." Edward raised his eyebrows, gave me a half-smile and said, "But, of course, that was only in the eyes of the English.

"A pretty damp mountainside," he continued, as he raised his arm in an inclusive gesture. "Good for these sheep feeding here." I turned to look at the sheep, and he pointed upward, adding, "Here come a couple of Connemara ponies over the top of the mountain."

My efforts to come away with a lasting record of these sacred grounds were continually being thwarted by varying degrees of malfunction from all three of my cameras. The tape recorder I had used to document my views of the terrain was being sabotaged by the wind — the wind that always seemed to be at our backs, no matter which way we turned. The verbal descriptions of what we were doing, the emotions and the feelings of discovery were being overpowered and obliterated from the tape recordings by the force of the wind.

Were we intruding? Were we trying to capture a portion of someone's spirit that she didn't want to relinquish? My eyes darted, searching for a sign of anything physical that could be provoking this ill wind. I tucked all of my equipment into the backpack except for the one camera that was working at the moment, and eased down on a rock in an attempt to absorb more of the holiness of my surroundings.

We selected separate rocks to use for benches. As I tried to deal with the dreariness of daily living for these unfortunate people, I could feel myself withdrawing from Edward — from the present.

I looked down the hillside toward the roadway that continues on up toward Clifden. No matter where you stop to rest in Ireland, you are in the presence of magnificent beauty and you often feel compelled to take the time to behold its magic. This was no exception.

It is said that being unable to receive the sound of the human voice is the loneliest of all sensations. As we sat near the top of this mountain and reveled in the silence, serenity, and sadness of our surroundings, I did not miss the sound of the human voice. The Connemara landscape allows you to mentally travel back through ancient struggles and view the ruins that today remain untouched.

I admired the Irish for not responding to the need to destroy and rebuild. The softness of these people comes from being in unity with their heritage, their ancestry, and it has produced a purity, a charm, a richness all its own.

No matter how many invaders tried to control them, the intruders all found that you are unable to steal from another what you cannot touch. Their Celtic roots are firmly planted in the beauty and flow of unending circles. They believe that what you are, is what you have always been.

I turned to watch the two ponies making their way down the mountain toward us. The solemn stillness was

One legend of the Connemara Pony claims that when Galway had strong links to the Spanish, one of the Spanish Armada ships sank and some of the horses swam ashore.

The ginger-colored Connemara pony had not yet thawed from the stance she assumed when the dirt clod hit nearby. Her unflinching eyes were affixed to mine. The hair on the back of my neck bristled.

shattered when I cleared my throat and asked Edward about the history of the Connemara ponies.

Still using a voice of reverential regard for his surroundings, he replied, "One legend is that when Galway had strong links to the Spanish, one of the Spanish Armada ships sank, and some of the horses swam ashore. It is also said that in parts of northern Spain, there are horses quite similar to the Connemara pony. No one knows for sure how they came here — or when."

I admired their sleek coats and the slightly downsized scale of their bodies. They show great stamina by just surviving in an area that consists mostly of raw beauty, lakes, solid-limestone mountains and bog land.

"I wish they would share some of their grit with me." I wasn't sure whether I said this aloud or not.

Edward broke another long silence by asking if I was ready to start back down the mountain. My reply was a simple, "No." He said there was a chill to his back. I scooted to one side of my big boulder and invited him to join me.

He moved, then said, "This is much better, being away from that wind." Was there more to the chill of the wind than we were willing to recognize?

I watched the grace of these matchless specimens from the animal world as they made their sure-footed and deliberate way down the mountain. Their descent carefully followed the contour of the rocky hillside. It was becoming more apparent that the two of us were to be their ultimate destination.

"Are you uncomfortable with this at all?" Edward asked.

I took a deep breath, released it slowly, and confessed, "I am not completely at ease."

As the ponies came around the boulders we were using for a windbreak, Edward plucked a piece of turf from the shallow root system atop the rocky formation and tossed it in their direction.

The tawny-colored mare bristled, froze, and flared her nostrils. I saw the muscles in her foreleg ripple as she gave a slight toss to her ginger-tinged mane. She barely diverted her steady gaze to send a fleeting message to Edward that he was not to be a part of this.

Unlike most horses, her eyes were positioned in her head at an angle that allowed her to connect her full gaze directly with mine. She was no longer burning into my brain but, instead, was weaving gossamer, hypnotic charms that began to enfold my very being.

I barely heard Edward ask, "Are you okay?"

"Still not sure," I whispered.

In an attempt to dilute the tension, he started to talk in his low, slow, calm voice. "These two look so much alike in their facial structure, I am guessing they are mother and daughter."

I did not take the time right then to ponder the complexities of a man who could recognize family traits in the faces of ponies.

As a form of gentle recognition, Edward acknowledged the mother pony's demands by turning his attention to her daughter. The curiosity of the jet-black youngster brought her close enough to sniff my backpack, which I had abandoned a couple of feet in front of us.

The tawny mother had not yet thawed from the stance she assumed when the dirt clod hit nearby. Her unflinching eyes were still affixed to mine. The hair on the back of my neck bristled just a little.

I felt yet another flicker in my composure. I wished she would break eye contact long enough for me to check and see if their hooves had been shod. The last of my uneasiness might be calmed if I knew whether I was dealing with wild horses or tame.

She did not blink. Nor did I.

In one brief enchanted moment I felt my remaining fears crumble and fall away. Both ponies were concentrating on me so intently now that I began to feel their trust in me growing — or was it my trust in them? I felt my spirit open to a complete and honest exchange with all forms of nature around me, granting me a calm that anointed me.

As the mother began to walk forward, Edward slowly raised his hand, placing it between her eyes and mine. I guessed that he still felt a need to protect me by trying to break the tension that locked us.

I whispered "I am okay." He lowered his hand, and she took two more steps, coming well within a measurement of inches. We were almost nose to nose. Neither of us lost eye contact during the brief interruption, but both of our expressions had changed.

I could no longer hear the thunderous thump-thump of my pulse pounding in my ears. I raised my hand as she lowered her head, allowing me to stroke her nose. When I finished, she nodded to me. She dipped her head three distinct and separate times, breaking our spell.

The wind stopped.

In unison, the ponies turned away from each other treading the outline of a perfect heart. At the point of the heart, they came together again and walked back up the mountain just as slowly as they had come, never looking back. I watched them disappear over the top. They were only gone from my vision, not from my life.

I felt some degree of peace in my emotional struggles with my O'Hagertys by visiting and experiencing the desolation of this mystifying famine village called Lettercraff.

My pony messenger led me to better understand how my broken spirit longed for a renewed richness of life, which promised to be awakened by my haunting need to know more about my past.

I wondered if the tawny pony with the mane the color of ginger had come to deliver a message to me from the little people who live under the ground, or was she perhaps one of them?

You must be a believer to know for sure.

chapzer four

"OH, TAKE A GOOD LOOK at that, now would you?" I sounded so Irish to myself that I couldn't suppress a half-hearted smile. I loved it when Daddy did that, too. Nothing in this world made him more proud than being Irish.

"Let's go take a look."

"But we just sat down," Dennis teased. "You're the one who was too tired to walk any farther."

I squinted for a better view of the vintage bus sliding into a parking place on the far side of the square.

Dennis and I were back on our feet and ambling over for what would normally have been the stroke of approval for anything that stands out to a tourist — the inevitable snapshot. However, my camera remained nestled in the bottom of my backpack, undisturbed.

"What do you think? Fifty years old?" I asked.

"How should I know? You're the only one around here old enough to make that judgment call," Dennis replied.

His smart remark caused me to take a backhanded swipe at his head, as he ducked just out of my reach. He grinned and continued to search the bus schedule.

We strolled across the gently flowing pathways that almost demanded you honor them, by staying off the manicured verdant grass of John F. Kennedy Park. Those not using the sidewalks were a dozen schoolboys venting some of their pent-up energy during their lunch break. It wasn't evident whether they were playing an organized game, or just wrestling, but they were toughing it out to a struggle, either way. Men watching the boys told me by their expressions that they were reliving a part of their own past. A few office workers had thought far enough ahead to bring along a blanket to spread on the grass. The Irish soak up their sunshine whenever they can get it. The neatness of the oversized planters that housed an assortment of flowers bursting with color were like beacons inviting the visitors to help maintain the beauty of Eyre Square, nestled here in the heart of downtown Galway.

As we made our way to the far side of the square for a closer inspection of the bus, Dennis told me, "I think we made a big mistake scheduling this trip so late in the season. Nothing seems to be working to our advantage."

"All I really care about at this point is seeing the rest of Connemara and finding our way up to Clifden."

"Yeah, I know. And if we don't get to Clifden, we won't be able to dig around in some dusty old library. What a terrible loss that would be."

"Well, obviously not for you, but I want to see if we can find something about our O'Hagerty roots while we're this close. This may be my last trip across the big pond and, if I don't do it while I am here, I know you won't do it after I go back home."

Edward had taken me through a part of Connemara yesterday when we visited Lettercraff. It had been quite an outstanding day in its own right, but it was still a famine village. I returned to the townhouse completely drained. Dennis commented on my obvious exhaustion, and I allowed him to think it was still jet lag.

Not since my transition into adulthood have I ever been able to share with another human being what really goes on deep inside of me. Last night I would have traded my entire worth for someone not only to listen to me, but also to hear me. There is such a big difference between listening and hearing. I longed for someone to share the heartbreak of my experience.

I knew I was experiencing a life-changing event at the time it was taking place. Usually, things of this magnitude surface in your mind and take their proper place through clouded hindsight. Only Edward will ever know how painful — yet exhilarating — my day had been. I descended that mountain an entirely different person from the one who had climbed it.

Dennis brought me back to Eyre Square, saying, "You know, if we hadn't already paid for our passage to the Aran Islands for tomorrow, we could go to Clifden then, but the bus only runs on Thursdays once the tourist season is past."

Dennis continued to search the bus schedule as we walked. It must be the age difference that allows him to be able to walk and read at the same time.

"Even if we could exchange the boat passage, we couldn't move the Aran Islands trip to Friday, because I bought tickets to tour the Burren on Friday," I told him.

"And these are both full-day trips," he added.

I tried to throw it off casually by saying, "Well, if I don't make it to Connemara this trip, it means that I will have to come back again next year to do our search for the O'Hagertys. I still would like to find some documentation to confirm their existence — something tangible — other than the two of us."

His expression brightened to a smile. "I was hoping you weren't serious when you told me this ocean crossing would be your last."

I was still having problems making firm commitments now that I was on my own. Independent decision making had never been difficult for me in the past, and it baffled me why it continued to be such a problem.

I tried to change the subject. "You know, before I came to Ireland, I made one promise to myself and that was to not be a typical tourist this trip. I am looking for something more meaningful."

Dennis graciously let me switch subjects by saying, "First, explain to me what a 'typical tourist' is and then tell me what that other thing might be that you are looking for. Could it be like a new husband, maybe?"

I did not try to hide my anger with him. His humor is occasionally caustic and sometimes abrasive, but most times it is well placed and for good reason. He missed his mark with this one.

"It seems to me that typical tourists observe the beauty of their surroundings through the confines of a camera lens, missing the impact the environment can make on the soul. They also listen to tour guides recite words from a notebook that probably someone else wrote for them.

"That is what was so different about my tour yesterday. It was only one-on-one with this Irishman visiting with me, not performing for the masses."

I looked directly into Dennis' face and tried to cover my irritation with him, but I could not offer him a smile. "And I don't know what that other thing is, but I know I haven't found it, yet. One thing I do know for sure is that it certainly is not a new husband. I have had my one and only. Of that, I am sure."

"Well, so far, you haven't done very well sticking with your other firm decision. Just this morning, I counted the rolls of exposed film you have already stacked next to the salt and pepper on the breakfast table," he said.

"Can I count on you coming back again next year?"

I gave him a shrug and looked away. I caught him staring at me, and he just couldn't leave well enough alone.

"Never say never," he added. "How do you know you will never remarry?"

"I know because the one who could entice me at this point in my life doesn't exist."

"How do you know he doesn't exist?" Dennis asked. "Describe him. And please try not to make this perfect person sound as if you're describing me, okay?"

"Well, that should be easy enough." I stopped walking and reflected for a few seconds before I could even begin to talk.

"He must have a genuinely tender nature, a unique bond with children, compassion for the feelings of others, and an impeccably balanced sense of humor." I stopped again to collect more thoughts.

"Is that it?" Dennis asked.

I looked at him again without actually seeing him, then continued. "He would have to display an appetite for simplicity while a cluttered and very complex world clatters about him. Anyone would be able to instantly recognize the pleasure he derives from life itself."

"Okay, that's enough," Dennis covered his ears with his one free hand and the bus schedule.

"No, now come on. You asked, so be quiet and listen.

"He would be someone who is perfectly happy with his profession, his family, his ancestry, and his sense of self," I continued. "He would be an earnest, industrious, hard worker, without displaying the negative sides of ambition. He would be attentive to those around him without being solicitous. He would set aside his own pleasures to tend to the comforts of others. And the kindness in his eyes would reveal the gentleness of his soul. He would be a generous giver of himself and a gracious receiver from others. People seldom possess both traits."

"Okay, okay! Stop! I asked you not to describe me,"

Dennis frowned at me, while at the same time giving me that devilish grin of his.

"And you know as well as I, that this person does not walk on the face of this earth — male or female — and that includes you, bucko. So, I am safe in telling you that there will never be a second husband for me."

"Okay, so you're not looking for a husband. Exactly what is this dream you have — this other thing that you haven't found, yet?"

I could not believe he left himself wide open for this one. He must be tired.

"Well, now, let's think about this for a minute. If I could answer that question, would I still be looking for it?"

The look on his face told me that he also couldn't believe he had left himself open for that one. He responded with a sheepish, "Touche."

Actually, I did know the dream I was searching for, but I have never been able to crack the facade behind which I have lived my entire adult life; the self-assured, sometimes aloof, professional shell that protects all of my true feelings.

I have only allowed one person to know that I even possess any depth or sensitivity in my emotions and that was just for a brief moment in time. I would like to be able to share my feelings with someone special again, but I have never been able to trust another person enough to relate what dwells deep down inside of me. It made me feel so vulnerable when I handed another person that kind of information. It was like offering them unlimited entitlements that they could use against me at their discretion. I have been too fearful to hand over that kind of power to anyone.

At this particular time in my life, I carry a secret dream to walk barefoot through a field of wildflowers, pace my stride and sway to the roar of the sea, and fill my lungs with the earthy smell of burning turf swirling from the chimney of a nearby cottage. I want to get to know an Irish family and experience a portion of their tenderness as they wrap their arms around me and embrace me. I want to listen to the warmth of their soft-spoken brogue, peppered with humor and song.

If this can never be, I would settle for being in a movie, starring that incredible human being I just described. It would star other Irish people like Maureen O'Hara, Barry Fitzgerald — and me. I want to become a part of these people. Not as a visitor, but as one of them.

Aloud, I said, "I would really like to get to know an Irish family. I want to know what they think, what they say to each other, the mechanics of their family structure."

"The only way you are going to do that is to break your barrier on the Bed and Breakfast rule next year."

"Nope. Can't do that."

Dennis knew only too well that I still have a great deal of trouble sleeping. I get up all hours of the night to wander around, go back to bed, read, toss, turn, and get up again. The B&B hostess would evict me the first time I tried to make a 3 a.m. pot of coffee. But I would still love to blend into a family just to share with them and know what it feels like to be a part of their uncomplicated way of life.

One of the first things I notice each time I visit Ireland is the apparent happiness and contentment of their children. They almost never display bad humor or bad manners; at least not in public. I have mixed among crowds for days without hearing a baby cry or a child whine. I have yet to see one throw a tantrum.

I want to understand the love these people have for their young and for each other that provides such richness in their lives.

It is that same sensitivity about them that shows in their

eyes and in their actions toward complete strangers. A love and tenderness I may never be able to experience. I need to know if I am, or ever will be, capable of embracing these feelings again.

I don't just want to stop looking through the eyes of the visitor. I want to become a player in a former time and see my beginnings, while trying to visualize and understand how I evolved into the person I am today. I have both gradually, then abruptly, become aware of my own mortality and I want to find myself before I am lost to this world forever.

We reached the far side of Eyre Square and crossed the street in the middle of the block. We brushed by the front of the big, green bus, admiring its age, style and grace, its shiny green paint and chrome trim.

The Irishman sitting nearby glanced up at us from under his snapped-brim, brown tweed cap, which he had cocked just a little to the right of center. He was seated on a folding stool — one we Americans call a campstool — a few feet back from the open door of the bus. He was leaning against the brick storefront, writing in a small, dog-eared spiral notebook. He stopped writing, stood, and showed us how he had come by those crow's-feet, displaying his warm smile. He seemed to revel in the aura of admiration we were displaying toward his bus.

I had been trying to imagine how this bus had lived her life up to this moment. I wanted to know about some of her unique passengers. Who had owned her all of these years? Who had taken such loving care of her that she still shone like a brand-new coin that had become someone's treasure? Her character lines were not unlike those of an aging matriarch, clutching her shirttail link to royalty with a vise-like grip. I was able to fully appreciate her beauty and grace, which still glistened through her outdated style.

"Would you be interested in taking the afternoon tour?"

Hugh Ryan

the Irishman asked.

I answered his question with a question so quickly that it made me sound as if he had caught me lurking around in the past and private life of his beloved bus. "Do you go to Clifden?" I asked.

"Close, but I am sorry, I don't go that far," he replied with a smile.

"How far do you go?" I asked.

"I only go as far as Maam Cross," he replied, which meant nothing to me.

"I've tried every way I know to get to Clifden, up in the Connemara region, but I can't find a way to get there from here, now that the buses don't run there every day."

"Close doesn't count?"

"How close is close?" I asked. "Exactly where is Maam Cross?"

He spoke the single word "Connemara" as he used the tip of his pen to point to the sign above the bus windshield, which read "Connemara Bus."

He told me, "This tour, which lasts about four hours, will take you through a good portion of the Connemara region. I will take you on a trip through the past. The tour will take you through a portion of my grandfather's bus route. My grandfather drove the original Connemara Bus, you see, back in 1932."

I broke into a mirror image of his incredibly warm smile and replied without even consulting Dennis. "Yes, we would like to take your tour."

The vintage green bus stirred a mental image of an Ireland in a different day and time. It was bringing me at least to the rim of discovery of what used to be — the Ireland I had been searching for since I stepped off the plane. I walked away from the bus while Dennis visited with the Irishman and paid for our tickets.

I had already owned up to the fact that playing the part of the tourist would not help me repair the damage that had ripped my psyche. I needed more. I was still seeking the connector that would tell me why I thought just being in Ireland would give me the strength to work my way through my dreary future.

I have repeatedly closed my eyes and tried to sort out my past, present and future. The one thing I can see clearly in my mind's eye is my transparent body being drawn toward white smoke, eventually being absorbed into a haze that envelops me in a warm and loving cushion of comfort. I keep hoping it will be the beginning of what will help me understand my past and sort through the burdens of my new responsibilities, but that haze never clears.

The only logic I have been able to attach to this dream is that a good turf fire is easily recognized by the purity of the white smoke that this earthen log emits. Maybe I need to focus on the white smoke in my life. That might force me to the crossroad where I will be able to rekindle my life and begin it anew — or perhaps watch it dwindle and maybe even flicker to an end.

Intellectually, I know that my spirit and my physical body cannot survive without me being an active participant. In order to survive, I have to concentrate on being a willing contributor to a new way of life. I need to see if there is even a smoldering ember left in me that can create enough smoke to nurture a flame of expectancy again. I have to concentrate on whether I want to go on living — and if so, how?

Perhaps this lovely old bus, the Connemara Bus, could lead me down my pathway of renewal.

I watched the man hand Dennis our tickets and a couple of brochures. I heard him say, "I'll be looking forward to seeing you a little before two o'clock this afternoon. The bus will be parked right down this hill in front of the Tourist Office."

As Dennis fell in step with me, we walked off and I nudged him. He could see how pleased I was to be going to Connemara, and we both started to laugh like fools. I hoped the bus driver didn't think we were laughing at him.

Dennis and I sometimes do not even need to talk when we are together. We just nod and are able to see the same funny or ironic side of things, and this was no exception. I caught myself smiling as I walked along, reading the brochure.

Look at me! I am reading and walking at the same time.

chapter five

SO, HERE I WAS, preparing to seek my solace in the rocky, rolling hills of Connemara, located in the province of Connacht, which includes the counties of Galway, Mayo, Roscommon, Sligo and Leitrim. This western coastal area extends south from Killary Harbour almost to the city of Galway and from the western shore of Lough Corrib to the Atlantic Ocean, which the Irish commonly refer to as "the sea."

Researching for my trip, I had read that when the Ice Age finally released its grip on this land, Connemara's complex geology evolved into a mountainous area and was ultimately enriched by flora and fauna. This lush floriation enabled Connemara to become known as one of Europe's most aesthetically appealing and interestingly complex landscapes.

Christians settled in this area during the 6th century, followed by Vikings in the 9th and 10th centuries.

As recently as 1947, the body of a fully clothed Viking warrior was discovered near Clifden, with his shield, dagger, spear and sword lying beside him.

The earliest known find was near Oughterard and is believed to be a Bann Flake, which looked much like an arrowhead that had been used by nomadic hunters and gatherers. This find is estimated to be between 5,000 and 7,000 years old.

It only took me one full day to see that the western

area is drenched in the perfect mix of mist and mystical elegance. It blends a variety of hues, mostly borrowed from Ireland's forty shades of green, enhanced by an occasional splash of wild heather, lavender, rhododendron, fuchsia, or flowering mint.

I was stirred by the fact that the Great Artist Himself blended these appealing creations from His palette of colors. Just when I think I will never find a more perfect vision, He airbrushes it with an ethereal haze or a gentle rain shower, and there it is, even more perfect.

Some of the Irish people, but only those who live on the west coast, make a little sound as if they are catching their breath, not unlike the involuntary gasp of a child after a good cry.

I noticed that the driver of the Connemara Bus had done that when he was talking with us that morning. After we parted his company, I asked Dennis to identify this sound for me, and he said that as nearly as he could tell, it is a nonverbal expression of extreme approval.

That may be one explanation, but I believe another might be their unwitting response to the daily exposure of the exquisite natural elegance of where they live.

I was absolutely sure that I was where I should be and going where I should be going, on that very day.

Even though the Connemara Bus would not take me all of the way to Clifden or County Mayo, it might be as close as I was going to get to the home of my great-grandfather and his family — at least on this trip.

chapter six

I PULLED MY CHEEK AWAY from the cool glass of the windowpane, and the darkness from the clouds allowed my reflection to bounce right back at me. I watched the rivulets of raindrops racing down the outside of the glass, and they looked like tears on my face. I wondered if this was what my soul looked like.

Almost mocking my mood swings, the shower started, then stopped; the clouds blew over and the sun appeared again.

This was another amazing thing about the Irish. They pay rain no mind. They simply take it in their stride and go about their business of enjoying life. The clouds roll by, the sun shines down, and the Irish have not even paused for the weather.

I like to walk, especially in Ireland. The majority of the people are not as reliant on the automobile as we Americans are. When I stopped to rest and was unable to find an empty park bench, I asked permission to share with someone. The Irish response was always friendly and usually followed by a weather comment, "It's a lovely gray day" or "It's a lovely damp day." Then, on fair and sunny days, I would hear them give credit where credit is due, with variations of a standard comment in Ireland, "It's a grand soft day, thanks be to God."

I glanced up at the clock at the front of the green bus,

then at my watch. The clock was running slow. Just as my watch said it was time for our tour to begin, the driver stepped on board the bus, still wearing his same schoolboy smile, and introduced himself.

"Hello. My name is Hugh Ryan. I am the owner of this bus and I am also the driver. We're going to spend the afternoon together, so let's get acquainted." He asked for our first names and from where we hailed.

He started with Ruthie, a bubbly young woman who settled into the very front seat, ahead of the door, to share the windshield view with the driver. She turned around to face us and said, "Hi! My name is Ruthie and I am from Australia. I have been backpacking alone for the past two months. Ireland is my last country, and Galway is my last city before returning home. Tomorrow I am off to Shannon Airport to go home and then be off to college about ten days from now." It appeared obvious that Ruthie would enjoy whatever she happened to be doing at any given moment.

Hugh turned and looked at the young man sitting in the first seat behind the stairwell to the door.

"Ted from England," was all he offered. He returned to his intense investigation of the sidewalk right outside the bus window.

Lily introduced herself and her two adult daughters, whom she forgot to name, hopefully not at birth, but just for today. She said they were from England, also. "We only arrived in Galway this morning, and have come over to meet my brother, who is sitting across the aisle here." She reached across to touch his arm. "I am originally from Ireland, but moved to London when I married, and I am glad to be home again. My visits have been too few."

Mabel introduced herself, her daughter, Mona, and Mona's son, Kevin. They were from California.

Next was Michael from Pennsylvania, who appeared

to be a serious challenge to Ted from England, vying for the crown to adorn the King of Shyness.

Across the aisle was "Pete from New Jersey. This is not my first trip to Ireland and neither is it going to be my last." Pete slapped the young man ahead of him on the shoulder and said, "You're up."

"Andrew from Pennsylvania. Just call me 'Drew.' "

Hugh walked part way up the aisle with his right hand pointing to Michael from Pennsylvania, and his left hand pointing to Drew and said, "You two are from the same state. Do you know each other?"

Everyone turned to look and laughed. Michael and Drew looked almost like twins. The biggest difference was just a smidgen more of brown mixed in with Drew's auburn hair.

Drew laughed, too, saying, "Yes, Mike is my brother."

Still sober as a judge, Mike glanced at Drew as he talked, almost as if to guard against his brother saying more than he should.

Hugh pointed to Pete and asked if the three of them were all traveling together.

Pete spoke up and said, "I only met Mike and Drew last night. We kept running into each other while we were looking for a place to stay the night. We finally wound up in the same hostel. Regular rooms are still pretty scarce for being so late in the season."

Drew nodded in agreement.

Hugh backed up to greet the girl in the seat directly in front of Drew. She told us that she was Pia from Switzerland.

Next, Lily's brother identified himself as "Paul from Michigan."

When my turn came, I simply stated, "Ann, from the States." I didn't figure anyone would be interested in the fact that I was in Galway, seeking any available avenue of escape from the harshness of my own reality. Early on, I had given some thought to going back to Dunmore East, on the southeast coast to try and recapture the good times we once experienced there. My husband, our daughter, our son, a friend, my brother, and I spent two weeks in a holiday house on the coast of the Irish Sea. Even though these were wonderful memories, I wisely chose the opposite side of the country to launch yet one more new beginning.

Hugh waited to see if I was going to say anything more, then backed up to the seat ahead of me.

"Dennis, from Dublin," he said.

To keep from appearing like two more shy ones, I reached around the back of his seat, patted him on the arm and said, "Dennis from Dublin sounds like a song title."

Tom from Michigan started humming, "I think I know that one."

"Go, Tom, go!" Dennis urged, tapping his foot and slapping his leg.

Hugh laughed and moved on to the young woman seated ahead of Dennis, and here was "Lee, from Japan."

Hugh smiled and extended his hands, palms up, and said, "Welcome to the Connemara Bus, all of you."

Hugh was preparing to slide into the driver's seat, when we heard a screech, a shattering crash of glass, then the grinding and tangling twists of metals, all followed by a horn stuck in the blaring position. Hugh bounced back up to his feet and said, "I do hope they missed the bus altogether."

Right outside my window, I watched the two drivers slowly climb out of their cars, glance at each other, then silently inspect the damage.

Oh, boy! Shades of my childhood. Just before my daddy would initiate another one of his donnybrooks, someone would shout the words, "Jimmy's got his Irish up," which meant that the fight was about to begin. I could still hear the words.

The evening Daddy came home from work and announced that he had just been involved in his first automobile accident caused my mother's eyebrows to shoot straight up into her hairline. She questioned the accuracy of his numbering system, and Daddy admitted that he had probably been involved in 10 or 12 wrecks, but this truly was his first accident.

What's not to understand about that? Daddy's numbering system made sense to me. Dealing with justice can sometimes be very costly.

I watched out my bus window to see who was going to deliver the first punch. The two men faced each other in a civilized manner, and it was a good minute or two before they started punctuating their conversation with controlled gestures, while still talking only one at a time.

Daddy might have already thrown his second punch by now had it even been necessary.

So as not to let this dampen our trip, Hugh watched the two men walk away and said, "They're probably going somewhere to discuss the problem over a pint. While we wait for whatever is going to happen next, let me tell you a little about the bus.

"Just a few years back, I made the decision to recreate a good portion of my grandfather's bus route through Connemara, which is where it gets its name, the Connemara Bus.

"As you can see, the bus is specially designed for tourists. This one is fancier than the original, and the seats are much softer," which made almost everyone laugh as we readjusted our weight to test the comfort of our sitters on the rather firm seats.

"At least we have upholstered seats," Hugh laughed, then continued, "as opposed to the previous wooden bench version. Now, aren't we all glad for that? The bus-wide bench from which my grandfather, Andrew Ferguson, drove his bus is now a single, upholstered seat on the right, with a double upholstered seat on the left, where Ruthie is sitting.

"More differences between our bus and Andrew's bus are, for the most part, the standard ones you find between a regular and a deluxe model. Our bus has small lamps attached to the posts between the windows, which the original bus did not have. Of course, you'd have to get pretty close to these lamps to do any reading after dark. And if you apply some muscle to the chrome cranks, the windows will roll down, as well."

Hugh glanced at his wristwatch, stooped forward to look out the window, and we continued to wait. None of the passengers appeared to be worried about the time.

"Neither of the drivers seem to be anywhere nearby. If they are planning their strategy, I hope it isn't complicated enough to order a second pint. I am also more than a little grateful that they decided to just hit each other and not us, too. My grandfather drove his Connemara Bus 640,000 miles without putting a scratch on it, and I would like to do the same with this one," he added.

"Our departure is going to suffer a little delay, because we seem to be hemmed in, right where we sit. So, while we wait, I may as well tell you more about my grandfather and the bus.

"For many years, my grandfather drove the original Connemara Bus, bringing the rural people who lived in the isolated parts of Connemara to market on Saturday.

"Andrew was the first independent bus driver in Connemara. When he obtained his Omnibus license, one of the stipulations for this particular type of license was that you must have a conductor to help people on and off of the bus. So, as young lads, my two older brothers and I all served on the original Connemara Bus as conductors to assist Andrew's passengers.

"Connie, my oldest brother, didn't last very long, because he would much rather be reading a book or studying.

"My next oldest brother, Liam, fit into his role quite well. He served the longest. In fact, I couldn't wait for him to move on to a regular job so I could become the conductor. I only got to work with my grandfather for about five years before he retired, just before he turned 80 years of age. Those were years I will always remember. He was a wonderful man, and those who knew him considered him to be a kind, gentle, caring man, as well as a good friend and neighbor.

"Andrew's bus was considered to be the lifeline between those rural people and, literally, the rest of the world. If it hadn't been for him, many of those people would never have been able to leave their isolated farms and communities.

"The original bus was a Bedford 1932-OBW model, and this one is a Bedford 1949-OB Deluxe model. Other than that, it is the same color, the same size, the same chassis, and the same four-speed crash-gear box, which you have to double clutch and then listen to it growl and complain. The six-cylinder engine runs on petrol. Top speed attained in the new bus is 47 miles per hour."

Hugh laughed and said, "Neither Liam, my brother who helps me drive this bus sometimes, nor myself have ever received a speeding ticket behind the wheel of the Bedford. Still, this is a speedier model than my grandfather's bus, for even though his top speed was 37 miles per hour, he only exceeded 30 miles per hour on one occasion. That was when he rushed a child to the hospital here in Galway city.

"Liam, who was the bus conductor on that particular Saturday morning, tells about the tinkers who frequently parked their caravans, staked their horses, pitched their tents, and made their camps near our little town of Oughterard. One family in particular was a very nice family, the Wards. John Ward was the King of the Tinkers. The tinkers would have a fight every year, and the winner of the fight was the King of the Tinkers for that year. John Ward won that title several times. He was a lovely man — a very quiet man."

Hugh's diametric descriptions made us laugh.

"John used to come on the bus now and again to Galway city. On this particular Saturday morning, Liam recalled, John came with his daughter, who was about 12 years of age, and John had to support her so she could walk.

"My grandfather asked, 'What is wrong with your girl?' Her father says, 'She has a touch of the flu and is not feeling well.' Andrew looked at her and said, 'No, there is something seriously wrong with that girl.' Liam says they got the girl and her father aboard and off they went straight away into Galway. Andrew didn't stop for any of his regular passengers, but went straight away to the hospital. Double pneumonia she had. Liam remembered that morning very well. So, it was Liam who was with Andrew the one and only time he drove his bus over 30 miles per hour."

Hugh continued telling us about the bus. "We have the same number of seats as the old bus. A few of the pieces on this bus have been replaced by pieces from my grandfather's bus."

The pride in his face let us know how Hugh felt about what he was doing with his life.

"After we make our first stop, and you come back aboard the bus, notice that this bus bears an oval metal plaque mounted here on the left side of the stairwell, as you enter. That plaque is its Public Service Vehicle plate: ZV-1460. My grandfather's PSV plaque was IM-5630, and instead of mounting it anywhere on his bus, he proudly pinned it to the outside of the brown canvas bag he wore

Connie Ryan (left), age 7, was Andrew Ferguson's first grandson to serve as conductor on the original Connemara Bus. Liam Ryan, age 6, anxiously awaited his turn.

Liam Ryan, age 10, was already working on the Connemara Bus when this school photo was taken. All three grandsons served only on Saturdays and during their summer holiday from school.

Hugh Ryan, age 5, could hardly wait for Liam to "get a regular job" so he could be the conductor on his grandfather's Connemara Bus. Hugh worked with his grandfather until they retired together. Andrew was nearly 80 years of age and Hugh had just turned 13. Andrew's youngest grandson, Anthony, never got to work as conductor.

L-R, Aidan Burke, age 7, Bernard Craven, age 6, and Hugh Ryan, age 8, using their hurley sticks as rifles. Andrew would park near the school and take the boys for a spin on the bus after their Saturday classes. Soon after this photo was taken, Hugh finally became the Connemara bus conductor.

strapped across his chest. It was in this canvas bag that he deposited the fares."

For the first time, Hugh's smile faded as he confided, "The fares are still a bit of a bothersome thing for me to talk about for, you see, my grandfather would never allow me to collect the fares. Not one time did he ever allow me to collect the fares. Liam had been allowed to collect the fares occasionally, but my grandfather never let me." This didn't keep Hugh from thinking of Andrew Ferguson as being less than a grand man — he was just never allowed to collect the fares.

Hugh showed a well-defined sense of pride each time he mentioned his grandfather. He must have loved him very much. I shared his close attachment to family.

Hugh looked at each of us, then came that smile creeping across his face again. He received chuckles from everyone — everyone but me, that is. I could see that he told us this story in jest, but in my precariously balanced emotional state, I felt sure I could see right through his smile to a hurt that hadn't yet mended.

Hugh stepped off the bus to see about the release of his bus from the prison in which it was placed by the locked automobiles.

The reappearance of the two drivers of the damaged autos finally released us from our curbside box. Hugh may have been correct about where they'd been, because they were laughing and talking like old school chums when they returned.

The cars were moved, Hugh settled into his seat and announced that we were finally on our way. He turned to Ruthie, seated to his left, and asked her if she would be responsible for starting the bus for the rest of the afternoon, because the starter switches were located closer to her knee than to his.

Hugh explained, "You turn the key, and when the ignition light comes on, then you pull on the starter.

"Andrew didn't have a Ruthie, so he used a shoelace. He would tie the two ends together, loop the lace over the starter knob, then put his finger in the loop and pull.

"I am sure he would rather have had a Ruthie, because there was a soft spot in Andrew's heart for hikers. Back then, hikers usually carried their national flag stuck in their rucksacks. He would always stop and offer them a ride with never a charge. He enjoyed visiting with them about their homeland, where they had been, where they were going."

Hugh returned Ruthie's smile, then told us, "I usually reserve this seat and this duty for the youngest person on the bus, but I asked Kevin from California and he declined the honor."

Hugh looked in the rearview mirror and assured Kevin that his decision was perfectly all right for him to make.

With that, everyone on the bus turned to look for Kevin only to see the top of his head disappearing as he slid down in his seat. I kept turning around to peek at him and finally got a smile from him.

When we departed Eyre Square, we were running just over 30 minutes behind in Hugh's regular schedule.

Hugh talked to us on his microphone as he drove.

"We start our tour out of the city of Galway and go by the docks of Galway Harbor. The bay is very shallow, and ships can only come in when the tide is high.

"The main fishing port in Galway is not in Galway Harbor, but is located in Rossaveel, which is on the northern shores of Galway Bay.

"As we head for Salthill, we will cross over the Corrib River on the Wolf Tone Bridge, but first we go by the Spanish Arch, which is part of the Old City Wall, built in 1584. It was named this because most of the ships tying up at the

The Spanish Arch is a part of the old city wall, built in 1584.

Beside the Spanish Arch is the Long Walk that leads out to the Atlantic Ocean.

This marble memorial located near the Wolf Tone Bridge, at the head of the Long Walk, reads: "On these shores around 1477 the Genoese sailor Cristoforo Columbo found sure signs of land beyond the Atlantic."

The area, known as Claddagh, is located opposite the Long Walk — across the Corrib River.

81

quayside were Spanish.

"This area here in front of the Jury Hotel was at one time the center of the old town of Galway and still today is known as the Fish Market.

"As we cross the river, here on the left is a famous part of the city, an area known as Claddagh. It has changed a lot over the years, for it used to be a village of thatched roof houses. In 1938, the city authorities demolished them for sanitary and health reasons, and it improved the city quite a lot. After the old cottages were destroyed and the open sewage was cleaned up, they built these current cottages.

"It was a unique part of the city. Actually, for many, many years it was outside the boundaries of the city itself. The people of Claddagh were involved in fishing, which was a big industry here that employed up to 2,500 people at one time.

"The Galway merchants allowed those who lived in Claddagh to cross over into the city and sell fish at the Fish Market in front of Jury's and near the Spanish Arch.

"You may also be familiar with the Claddagh ring. It is the people of this area who adopted the Claddagh ring as their betrothal and wedding ring. It is two hands clasping a heart surmounted by a crown. A number of jewelers here in Galway make the Claddagh ring and many people now wear it.

"This roadway will bring us up along Fair Hill, which is part of Claddagh. At the end of this road, we will come out overlooking Galway Bay. Across the bay is County Clare. We will have a nice view of the bay in a moment."

Hugh pulled up alongside some children from one of the schools in Fair Hill practicing a band formation in the middle of a side street.

"It looks like they are marching and practicing with the

cheerleaders today." Hugh tooted his horn and the students all waved those fingers that were not needed to make their musical instruments function.

We came to the end of the street that took us through Fair Hill, and Hugh said, "There is a brief glimpse of the sun shining on part of the bay. You can see that the bay is quite shallow, and there are quite a lot of rocks out there. Out here is an island, known as 'Mutton Island.' There is a ship waiting by it for the tide so it can enter the docks.

"We are looking south at the moment, and directly across the bay to an area known as the Burren. It is part of County Clare. 'Burren' comes from an Irish word known as Boireann and means 'a rocky place.' And that is exactly what it is — it is mostly limestone. It is a rocky area where botanists from all over the world come to study. Ireland stands in the path of both the prevailing westerly winds of the Atlantic and the warming currents of the Gulf Stream. Its unique weather finds unusual combinations of foliage growing right next to each other in the Burren.

"One story goes that when Oliver Cromwell came here to the west of Ireland, around 1652, he sent one of his officers over to County Clare on a fact-finding mission. Upon his return, his report was: 'I could not find a tree tall enough or straight enough from which to hang a man, the water was much too shallow to drown a man, and the ground was so dense with rock and clay that you could not bury a man.'

"Now, if you have been to the Burren, that is exactly what you have seen. Most of the water over there is underground. The limestone is quite soft — a very porous rock — so the water doesn't lodge on the surface. It is mostly underground caves and rivers."

Hugh turned the corner to the west, and we listened as the bus complained about getting us back up to speed again.

"On a clear day off the coast of Galway, sometimes you can see the Aran Islands. They are about 35 miles offshore and there are three islands: Inismor, which is the big island; Inismaan, which is the middle island; and Inisheer, the westerly island.

Now, you might be wondering, where are they? Well, they are out in the ocean and some days you can see them but, I am sorry, it is not this day. The clouds have moved in but they are out there on the horizon, off the coast of Galway and in County Clare.

"Those who have been to the Aran Islands have heard the people speaking Gaelic — speaking Irish. There are approximately 1,500 families living on the Aran Islands, and most of the people who live there speak Irish as their first language. You will find that in different parts of Connemara, on the mainland, as well.

"I live in Connemara myself, in a place called the parish of Moycullen. We also have strong links to the Irish language.

"Here is the beach on our left, known as Grattan Road Beach. The tide is coming in and by the time we get back this evening, it will be pretty well up. The rise will be about 10 feet. Some of the spring tides will be as high as 12 feet.

"We are passing The Seapoint, which used to serve as a dance hall. Now it has a bingo hall, a casino, and other recreational facilities.

"My grandfather used to bring friends and neighbors into town on a Sunday evening to dances held at The Seapoint and also at The Hanger.

"We're going to stop here at the Tourist Office at Salthill to pick up some passengers, then I will tell you more about the bus and the tour."

Six new passengers came aboard and sat down without introducing themselves. Those already on the bus bid them welcome, but Hugh did not go through the introductions again. It may have been a concern for time, even though he wasn't making any of us feel as if time was an issue.

Instead, he said, "My name is Hugh Ryan. I drive the Connemara Bus and I own the bus. The reason we are on an old bus is because today we will be traveling back in time.

"This bus was made by an English company and has been restored — not reproduced. It is a 1949 Bedford bus and is what they call a vintage bus."

Hugh said, "I don't want to embarrass anyone, but this is a topless bus, you see." He slid the roof open, shut it, and opened it again. He wound down one of the windows, and wound it back up again, then pointed out the bells for stopping the bus. He pressed one as he was demonstrating the features. It was a flat buzz that made everyone laugh.

He said, "Except for the chassis, the rest of the bus frame is made from a fine mahogany wood and it is put together with wood screws.

"From time to time, people ask where is the best place to sit on this bus. I tell them there is no best place. What you miss out of the window on one side you will have time to see out of the other side, for we don't go that fast. So, please sit anywhere you like. Except the driver's seat. I need that one. Feel free to move about to suit yourself. I want you to be comfortable.

"What we will be doing today is following the route that my grandfather used to drive. I will be telling you stories about him as we go along. My grandfather operated the original Connemara Bus. His name was Andrew Ferguson. Did anyone know him? No? Oftentimes someone will say they did. Just last week there was a lady who had moved to America many years ago. She was visiting here, and when I asked that question, she said she rode the Connemara Bus with Andrew when she was a little girl. She could remember sitting behind him and watching the back of his head and his old brown hat. He could be recognized from afar by his old brown hat.

"It is also not uncommon for older people to tell me that they met the person they married while riding the Connemara Bus.

"My grandfather, Andrew Ferguson, brought the people into Galway for 32 years, until he retired just before he turned 80 years of age. What we will be doing today is following the route that Andrew drove from 1932 to 1964. He brought the people to town to market so they could sell their chickens, ducks, eggs, homemade brown bread, freshly churned butter, and other forms of produce.

"I will be telling stories about him and the area — things that you might not know otherwise, for I come from the same part of Connemara, as well. I was brought up in the town of Oughterard and it is one of the towns we will be traveling through. We have several stops to make along the way.

"I think you will enjoy the afternoon. Hopefully, the weather will hold up." Hugh pointed to Ted from England and to Dennis from Dublin and said, "If it rains, you two have a job, if you don't mind. Your job is to close the roof. You stand behind it and give it a push. Okay?" They both nodded.

Hugh started to slip back into the driver's seat, but stopped in mid-air and turned to say, "The tour takes approximately four hours. We are leaving now, a little behind schedule, and should be back in Galway around 6:30 tonight. Now, the first thing I have to ask is, does anyone have a train or a bus to catch at 6:30? No? So, we are not in a hurry. As we Irish say, 'When God made time, He made plenty of it.' You are here in Ireland now, so take a rest. That makes it more comfortable for me as well, to know we are not in a hurry.

"I want you to know that you are all very welcome aboard the Connemara Bus.

"A quick head count now to make sure I have everyone. You can move around if you like. If you are not comfortable where you are, then pop into another seat. There is no one else getting on the bus this afternoon."

Tom from Michigan spoke up and asked, "When do we load the chickens and the ducks?"

Hugh laughed and replied, "The chickens and the ducks are loaded later on." He laughed again and said, "The poultry stop comes later on down the road.

"Okay? Here we go, now."

Just as he was about to pull away from the curb, a small group of people waved and shouted something to Hugh. He waved back and told us that they were part of a group that took the tour yesterday.

We drove a little farther down the street and he said, "Everyone smile, people are taking photos of the bus."

The vintage bus went through its series of growling and complaining, but before we left the promenade that runs along Galway Bay, Hugh turned on his microphone and said, "A friend of mine, Paddy Farrell, was out in a little fishing boat, called a 'curragh' last Monday, fishing for shark. Well, he caught a shark okay, but it was a little bit bigger than he was expecting. The shark spent the next two hours towing him around the bay. I have a little bulletin in my pocket to verify this if anyone feels a need to see it. Paddy is a neighbor of mine, and everybody was out waiting on the quay to see if he brought in this fish. He did, as a matter of fact. He brought in a 300-pound shark. It was over eight-feet long and weighed 18-stone. That shark gave Paddy a great tour of the bay — for hours. Paddy and his friend, Gerry Joyce, got the roller coaster ride of their lives just last Monday.

"Now, we are going on this road to connect up with the main road to Connemara. This is also the road that my grandfather traveled. Not from Salthill, but from Galway. Up near the university we will connect up with N59, the main road from Galway to Clifden.

"A lot of people remember my grandfather traveling in and out of Galway every week. Someone was telling me recently about the evening run, when he would be heading out of Galway after Saturday's market. There was a ladder on the back of the bus, you see, and some of the fellows from one part of the city known as Shantalla would hop on the ladder, and they would go up to the roof and get a spin up to their part of the city. Now, Andrew, being old, didn't know they were up on the top of the bus at all. That is, he didn't know it most of the time. Sometimes he would see people motion to him, and he would stop the bus and chase them away. I know several of the characters that used to do that. It was actually quite dangerous, but they would try it out anyway.

"For the visitors who are visiting Galway for the first time, Galway is the capital city in the west of Ireland. It has a population of around 65,000 people and is regarded as one of the fastest growing cities in western Europe. It is a university city and will also have the tag of being a young people's city. The students create an atmosphere here in Galway that is unique.

"Traditional cottages here in the city are not that common anymore, but there is one right here in front of us with the red door. Most of them are gone, now, along with the thatched roofs.

"This road is called St. Mary's Road, with St. Mary's College here on the left-hand side. This is an all-boy's boarding school and, out of the 800 pupils who are attending St. Mary's College, there are approximately 200 who are boarding at present. Priests from the diocese of the city of Galway run the school. The head priest there is Father O'Flaherty, a past pupil at the school, who originated from the Aran Islands himself. It is a tradition that many people from the Aran Islands send their sons to St. Mary's College. This is a secondary school for pupils age 12 to 18. Then, after secondary school, they go to the university, maybe. We also have girls' schools in the city and mixed schools as well.

"Just over to the right you will see the Galway Cathedral, the main Catholic church in Galway. A fine example of a modern cathedral, built with limestone, between 1957 and 1965.

"This part of the city is called Newcastle. We have the grounds of Galway Hospital on the left-hand side. It is a training hospital for doctors and nurses, and the medical students work on staff. It is known as the University College Hospital-Galway, even though it serves the counties of Galway, Mayo and Rahoon.

"Through the trees you can see the old university. This university dates back to 1845 and was originally commissioned by the Prime Minister of England, Sir Robert Peel. He was also responsible for establishing two other universities in Ireland: Queen's University-Belfast and University College-Cork, and they were originally known as 'the Queen's Colleges.' This one is the National University of Ireland-Galway, a new name that it got only recently. It has a student population of somewhere between 9,000 and 10,000 students. It is the only university here in the west of Ireland. You can see part of the university there behind the trees. The old university architecture was neo-Gothic with mock Tudor styling and it was built with limestone. You can see more of it there behind the trees again."

Hugh was right. The bus did not go so fast that you couldn't see everything he pointed out.

"Now, most of those students will be coming back to college later in the month of September and will be looking for accommodations around the city. They will be getting set soon for their academic year again, which runs from the month of September right through until the month of June.

"We are now on the main road out of the city that leads to Connemara. It is the Galway to Clifden Road — N59. Every week my grandfather would travel both in and out on this road several times.

"Saturday was market day on the bus, and most of the ladies would be bringing their farm items to be sold at the market at St. Nicholas Church in the center of the city. This would provide them with the money to bring flour, sugar and tea home again with them. I was told that one time a man got on the bus with a calf tied up in a bag. He put it under the seat and away they went into town.

"This area is known as the 'Corrib Village.' The students rent these apartments during the winter months, and the tourists rent them during the summer months. Coming is Dangan Hill. Once we get over this hill, we will be out in the countryside, but we are still in part of the Newcastle area. Behind us is the area known as 'Bushy Park.' And Bushy Park is in the parish of Rahoon.

"In a moment, down on our right, we will see the River Corrib, the river that runs through Galway. Trout and salmon are in this river. We will also see Lake Corrib or "Lough" Corrib. We will be going to see the lake later in the afternoon, and we will be stopping at a pier on the shores of Lough Corrib.

"Here on the left is a fine example of a traditional,

thatched roofed cottage. Now, there is a bachelor who lives there, and he told me that I should tell all of my lady passengers that he is available. His name is Jimmy Concannon. And Jimmy plays the fiddle quite well, so he would be able to serenade you to sleep. Any of the ladies aboard interested?"

Hugh looked in the rearview mirror at us, and I could see his eyes crinkling at the corners. I self-consciously became aware of the fact that I was grinning back at him. I looked around and saw that the rest of the ladies were, as well.

"No? Well, if you change your mind, you know where he lives.

"Down on the right we have the Corrib River again, and in the background you have the lake. Lough Corrib is the largest freshwater lake in the Irish Republic. It covers approximately 44,000 square acres. There are 365 islands — an island for every day of the year. Some of the islands are quite large, and there are people living on some of them. You can pick out some of the smaller islands if you look on your right. We'll see some of the larger ones later in the tour.

"Here on your right is Glenlo Abbey Hotel. It is a five-star hotel and is owned by a businessman from Salthill, Mr. John Burke."

Dennis turned in his seat to look at me. I flashed him a knowing grin. John Charles Burk was our maternal grandfather's name.

Hugh continued, "You can see they have their own golf course. There, you can see the tower of the old abbey. They appear to be doing quite well. They were very busy this summer. Sometimes they hire this bus as well for some of their events. This week the hotel had a group that I took to the racecourse. The race was cancelled because of the weather, but they held their function in a big marquee." I found out later that a "marquee" is called a "tent" back in the States.

"It cost £12 million to develop the abbey in 1991. It dates back originally to the late 1700s and was built and owned by one of the famous families of Galway city — the Blakes. The Blakes were one of the Tribes of Galway.

"Galway city is known as the City of the Tribes. There were fourteen ruling families that made up the Tribes of Galway. In alphabetical order, they were Athy, Blake, Bodkin, Browne, Darcy, Deane, Font, French, Joyce, Kirwan, Lynch, Martin, Morris, and Skerrett. These were the families that helped build medieval Galway into a major seaport.

"The Blakes were involved with Glenlo Abbey. Later in the trip we will see another house, called Ross House, originally owned by the Martin family, another one of the Tribes of Galway — The Martins of Ross. The roadway overlooking Ross House will be our first stop today.

"I will explain the location of Connemara, because people visiting Galway sometimes get confused about where it is. First of all, Connemara is a region of County Galway. If you look at a map of the county and see that you are west of Lough Corrib, you are more or less in Connemara. Now, even though Lough Corrib is on our right, we are not quite in Connemara, yet. We are in Rahoon, and this parish is in the diocese of the city of Galway.

"The next parish we pass through will be the parish of Moycullen. Moycullen will be the first parish on this road officially in the Connemara area. The dividing line between the parishes of Rahoon and Moycullen is this small bridge just ahead of us. On the left of it, you will see they are building a new bridge, and that new bridge will eventually define the beginning of Connemara.

"Over the bridge we go! So, we are now officially in

Connemara and the parish of Moycullen. Do you feel any different?"

Actually, I did. I had been anxious to get out into the countryside. I am not partial to any city, no matter how small or how historical it may be. I have always wanted to live out in the country or in a mountain cabin.

Hugh continued, "Moycullen parish has strong links with the Irish language. Many families here speak both Irish and English. Most speak fairly good Irish and it is taught mainly through the schools. This is our way of keeping the language alive. We have four schools in the parish and all four of them teach Gaelic, but only one teaches all subjects through the medium of the Irish language and that is Newtown School.

"In the year 2000 Newtown School will celebrate its 100th anniversary. They are planning a big celebration and will have the ladies dress up in the long flannel skirts, boots, and shawls, like they did when they rode the Connemara Bus with my grandfather. I have promised to donate the bus for that day. It should be a nice occasion.

"My grandfather encouraged young people to learn to speak English as well as Irish. He thought they would have a better chance of getting a job if they were fluent in both languages. He had a lot of contacts outside of the village and he was instrumental in helping young people find employment.

"You can see that a lot of the place names are also written in Irish. This is the tradition here in Moycullen to put the little stone plaques with the place names at the ends of the roads. They write it in Irish and then in English. See here on the left there is a marker with Tooreeny and Poulnaclough written in Irish, then in English. These are townlands on the side roads located in Moycullen.

"Within the parish there are a lot of little townlands. I

have lived in the parish of Moycullen, in the townland of Tullykyne for about 16 years, but I don't live on the main road of the village. I live down quite near Lough Corrib, four miles from the village, and you take this road here to the right.

"There may be 50 or 60 townlands that make up a whole parish."

Being from a large metropolitan area, I found it quite a contrast that Hugh would be giving us such detailed directions to his home. He made me feel as if we would all be welcome to drop by and visit him and his family.

I became even more aware of the Connemara transition as Hugh transported us away from the present. Our own interpretations and emotions provided an awareness of the beauty surrounding us, more than Hugh's words. He was providing the information and the framework, but we each brought our own history and used our own skills to transcend time and interweave our differences provided by our own backgrounds.

Like my daddy, I am very proud of my Irish heritage. Where I live in the United States, everyone claims to be Irish, if only on St. Patrick's Day. In America you are either Irish in your heart or Irish in your blood. I am blessed to be both.

I wonder why Americans feel this kinship. Our history books do not always portray the Irish in the best light, and today the only news we receive from our media is about the continuing struggles of Northern Ireland.

When I talk about my travels, my friends are amazed to learn that what they see on television does not include the entire country and that turmoil is not the sum total of Ireland. I have been asked if I feel safe when I visit here. I go out of my way to show that the Ireland I know is such a fair land. Even though their peace treaty is all we hear about,

Northern Ireland's beauty is primary.

Hugh caught my attention again by saying, "My grand-father would almost always wait for the ladies, no matter what was detaining them, but not the men. If the men were in a pub, Andrew would sometimes drive off and leave them. Now, it was different if they were courting a lady, for he would give them a chance — maybe ten, fifteen extra minutes — but not if they were delayed in a pub.

"Andrew had gone off and left Tommy Kelly so many times that some of his friends decided to help him out. When Andrew asked, 'Where's Tommy Kelly?' His friends spoke up and said that Tommy had met a fine young lady about a month ago and was now courting her. Andrew looked at them suspiciously and waited about an extra ten minutes before driving off and leaving him. When he found out the truth, he barred Tommy from the bus for a month.

"Here on the left we have a fine example of a granite stone wall. Granite wouldn't be very common in this particular area, for here it is mostly limestone, but sometimes people bring in the granite from farther away. These are the two types of stones found in Connemara — granite and limestone.

"Shortly, we will be coming to the village of Moycullen, but before we get there, there is another lake down here on our right. It is known as Ballyquirke. It is what we call a 'coarse' fishing lake. You will only find pike, perch, roach and bream in it.

"A lot of anglers come to western Ireland to fish in the lakes. In this area of Moycullen, there are a lot of small lakes like this one. It is a very popular area for the fishermen.

"I have been told that Lake Corrib is one of the 12 finest designated trout and salmon lakes in all of Europe. We are very lucky to have 10 of those 12 right here in Ireland, but Lake Corrib is the most famous and the biggest of those lakes."

As we approached the village of Moycullen, I glanced at those seated near me and saw their smiles matching mine. This is the warm, intimate little village that comes to mind when I think of an Irish townland.

"I told you earlier that Galway is one of the fastest growing cities in all of Europe. As Galway expands, so does the demand for housing in Moycullen. There are a lot of new houses going up in just the last four or five years. People like to live in the countryside and still be near the city.

"Not unlike any other village in Ireland, we have to have our share of pubs and they are all together here on the left-hand side: The Ferryman, Regans, and Lee's. Also there are nice restaurants here as well. The White Gables is on the left, along with some shops, and we have one local garage. The man who runs the garage, John Lydon, is a friend of mine.

"Also on the left, with nice welcoming flowers there in the windows with the nice lace curtains, we have the local police station. Pink is an unusual color for a police station, but there you have it. I don't think the inside is as attractive as the outside. I haven't been inside it too often, myself.

"The local policeman, Ray Lyons, is a friend of mine — sometimes. He's from County Mayo, but he can't help that. Ray is involved with Moycullen Football Club and I am involved with Killannin Football Club. We are great rivals. I have won — and lost — a few pounds off him over the years.

"Connemara Marble's factory is here on the left," Hugh told us. "Across the road here, Ambrose Joyce and his family have quite a lovely shop there as well.

"The green marble they use is quarried in the mountains of Connemara, and geologists estimate that it is about 500 million years old. The marble is cut and polished there in the Connemara Marble factory. The black marble is quarried on the shores of Galway Bay, and even though it is estimated to be 250 million years old, these quarries were only opened in the late 18th century.

"Ambrose Joyce's son, Michael, hand etches black marble jewelry with Celtic designs — designs that are taken from the Book of Kells.

"One of the finest examples of Connemara marble in the United States can be seen in the State Capitol Building in Harrisburg, Pennsylvania. The Senate Chamber and the Senate Post Office are lined with Connemara marble.

"Various Connemara marble quarries supplied the marble for the floors of the new Galway Cathedral, Shannon and Dublin airports, and many other public buildings and churches in Ireland.

"Villagers and visitors alike buy Connemara marble. During the summertime, the factory employs around 15 local young people.

"These stone walls here along the side of the road look old, but they're not, for they were built by the unemployed people of the area only last year."

It was hard for me to tell the difference between the old and the new. There is so much to be said for trying to maintain the old. I have never been an admirer of new and shiny.

"Most of the people in Moycullen are involved in farming, some full-time and some part-time, and the average-size farm in Moycullen will be about 30 acres. Some of their land will be quite hilly, like this on the left, and maybe some will be flatter. Some will be marshy, some bog, and there may be some good land as well.

"There are a lot of bed and breakfast inns in Moycullen. We also have three pubs and two priests."

Tom from Michigan asked, "No nuns?"

"No, no nuns — but we have lots of saints."

Hugh is quite good at bantering and getting laughs from his passengers, and he encourages it. He is very careful not to gain a laugh at someone else's expense.

"Here is another fine restaurant on the right-hand side, known as Drimcong House Restaurant owned by a chef from Limerick. His name is Jerry Galvin. Mr. Galvin is quite a famous chef. He has written several books about cooking, and he is very popular. He will close down now in another few weeks for the wintertime months and open again next February."

Mr. Galvin's restaurant looked like a country squire's estate, with its winding drive up to the house. We only caught a glimpse of nicely maintained outbuildings.

"We will pass on through the village and soon we will be stopping at Ross House in the next parish — the parish of Rosscahill."

It didn't take long to drive through the village. The younger children had already begun their classes, and as we made our way out the other side of the little village, school had just released its grip on them. Many of them turned toward the familiar sound of the bus, as each engaged in their own style of animated acknowledgment of Hugh. They were shouting messages to him as we drove by that only he could interpret. Hugh appeared to be somewhat embarrassed as he returned their waves, mumbling each of their names as we passed. He shyly admitted that all of this attention might have something to do with the fact that he coaches their football teams.

"A lot of these people still remember my grandfather and they still speak very highly of him, because he provided an important service to an awful lot of people. He would go into many areas of Connemara that were so isolated they would have no other way to get into the city.

Most of these people were trying to make an income by selling their goods at the market in Galway, and they were on the bus almost every week. They were bringing in one thing to sell and bringing home something else, so there was always bag and baggage on the bus.

"Another of the things I remember when I was young was all of the radio batteries. The old radios ran on batteries, and people used to bring them into the city and have them recharged.

"Earlier I mentioned Newtown National School, the school that is going to celebrate its 100th anniversary. Here it is. Children from the age of four to twelve attend this national school. The principal is a friend of mine. Her name is Eileen Anglim. There are three lady teachers there and they have 62 pupils. The Gaelic for Newtown is Baile Nua. You will see it written on a plaque there on the left-hand side.

"We still are in the parish of Moycullen.

"I have talked about the parishes and the towns today. Let me be a little more definitive. Ireland has two parts: there is Northern Ireland, which has six counties, and then the larger part called the Republic of Ireland, which has 26 counties. There are four provinces in Ireland. Within the provinces, there are counties, within the counties are parishes, within the parishes there are towns, then villages, then townlands.

"I live in the Republic of Ireland, in the province of Connacht, in the County of Galway, in the parish of Moycullen, in the townland of Tullykyne.

"Ahead, you will see a nice view of the mountains. There are two mountain ranges out there: the MaamTurks, which means, 'The Passage of the Wild Boar,' and the Twelve Pins. Together they are referred to as the Connemara Mountains. We are not always able to see the tops of the mountains, but it is quite clear at the moment.

"We have left the parish of Moycullen and are now in the parish of Rosscahill. Down on the right you will soon see Ross House, which was originally the ancestral home of the Martins of Ross. You can see the roof and the chimneys at the moment.

"The Martins had a very large estate, covering an area of approximately 20,000 acres of land, and it covered most of Connemara. It was one of the biggest estates in Ireland, and this was only one of their homes here — Ross House — or Ross Castle on the shores of Ross Lake. This may not look like a castle today, but it is. It is built of stone with cement walls and a hipped roof. In the mid-1700s, the Martins built this mansion over the ruins of the castle that was originally built in the 15th century by the O'Flahertys. The Martins' main home was at Ballynahinch Castle, about 30 miles away — near Clifden."

Hugh glanced in the rearview mirror at me when he mentioned Clifden.

"I'll just pull onto the left, because there's a load of cars in behind me and they are all trying to get out. I will pull off onto the grass, then I'll tell you a bit more about the house.

"We are going to stop at this lay-by and we'll have a rest or a smoker's stop, whichever you prefer to call it."

Hugh very carefully helped his passengers cross the road and once he got us safely delivered, we listened to him tell us more of the history of Ross Castle and the O'Flahertys, who for three centuries were the masters and rulers of Iar-Connacht (West Connaught). When he finished, he asked if there were any O'Flahertys on the tour. No one spoke up. He said, "Sometimes there are. I have to be careful.

"Not too long ago, I was about to tell the story of the O'Flaherty clan being the biggest threat to this side of the country, and about the inscription over the gate of the city erected in 1549, which read, 'From the ferocious O'Flahertys, God Lord deliver us.'

"I asked if there were any O'Flahertys on the tour, and one man on the bus spoke up and said he wasn't an O'Flaherty, but he was married to one. I'm not exactly sure why it was, but neither of us said anything more about the O'Flahertys.

"A lot of people from around this area knew about the Martins of Ross from older family members. Many of them had actually worked for the Ross family.

"One particular member of the Martin family, Richard Martin, at one stage in his life was a Member of Parliament, representing the west of Ireland. From a very early age, Richard was fond of animals. He was responsible for presenting a bill to Parliament in Westminster that protected animals, and eventually it was enacted and gave rise to the establishment of the Royal Society of Prevention of Cruelty to Animals — the RSPCA. Now, because of his involvement with this particular act and society, his fellow parliamentarians gave him the nickname, 'Humanity Dick.'

"It was not unusual during the famine years, between 1845 and 1849, for the Martins of Ross to have crowds of people gather at their house looking for food and refuge. The Martins of Ross were quite generous and sold most of their furniture to buy food to help feed the local people during the bleak years.

"There is a family living there right now from the United States — the state of Massachusetts. They made their money in the computer business in America and now live here in Ross House. They came here about 10 years ago and bought the house. He has spent a lot of money on the house since he bought it. Some say he has spent over a million pounds. Now, the amount of land he has with the house is not an awful lot, about 30 acres around the house, and he also has some land up on the hillside here on the left, some mountain land.

"They have built on some amenities for themselves. They have added a swimming pool at the back of the house, along with tennis courts and also stables for horses. They have a great love for ponies and horses. In particular, the lady has a great love for the Irish Connemara ponies. She has quite a few of them over there. Not too long ago she was actually kicked by a horse. She was in trouble for a while, but she has recovered now. Her husband has told her to stay away from the horses. There are some local men who help them look after the horses. They have cattle as well."

My heart began to race, thinking about my face to face with the Connemara ponies the day before. Perhaps I had been in more danger than I realized.

Hugh continued, "I have been in their home a few times. It is open to the public once a year, and usually, the money that is earned from the open day goes to one of the animal charities, like the Guide Dog's Association or the Cat and Dog's Home in the city.

"The Martins left here in the 1920s and the house was left idle for a number of years, until a Scotsman came to live in this house. His name was Chevas. He was a member of the Chevas Regal people who make the whiskey in Scotland, and I think he must have been a bit of a black sheep, because he lived here on his own and he never went back to Scotland, that I know. He spent most of his time here in Ross House.

"Mr. Chevas was a regular customer on my grandfather's bus. He and Andrew Ferguson would have a great chat, the two of them, there in the front of the Connemara Bus.

"Mr. Chevas would always stand out in a crowd. On a

Saturday morning when he was going to town, he would always dress up in his traditional tartan, and he wore a kilt and the sporran, the heavy woolen socks, and big boots. He would have a big walking stick and a funny hat with a feather out of it. Sometimes I would get a poke from his stick to move into the seat so he could sit down. He was a bit abrupt at times, but he was a great friend of my grandfather's.

"The main thing I remembered about him was his big hairy legs. He looked just like a gorilla.

"He used to travel into Galway to buy his groceries and he would always wait for Andrew Ferguson to take him. They were great friends. Mr. Chevas lived here for 30 years. He died in 1968, and his body was brought back to Scotland, where he is buried.

"It's a lovely sight for a house, sitting there on the shores of Ross Lake."

Hugh offered us another of his big grins and said, "We can't go there for tea, yet, but we might someday. I'm working on it."

Walking back to the bus, I learned that Lily from London and her stepbrother, Tom from Michigan, went their separate ways when they were old enough to leave the home of their parent and step-parent. The two of them had never gotten along very well, but after nearly 25 years, they decided it was time to at least become friends. Now they were finding that they had a lot of common interests and actually liked each other. I asked if she brought along her daughters as chaperones. She grinned at me using only one side of her mouth, then turned her head away and giggled.

We boarded the bus again and Hugh told us, "We are coming to Oughterard soon, which is my own hometown. And the town is particularly famous as an angler's town. A lot of fishermen come to Oughterard. Later, we will stop at the waterfall and see if we can see any salmon. There have been several sightings this week, and hopefully we will see some again today.

"This little building here on the left was the dance hall at one time. It is small, so you couldn't get many people into the hall, but there would be dancing out in the street as well.

"My grandfather decided to bring the people into the city for dances, or the cinema, or maybe the local pub on Sunday evenings. He did that for about 15 years, during the '50s and '60s.

"Here on the right, we have more nice examples of the limestone walls. These old stone walls are what we would call dry stone walls, where there would be no concrete or cement holding them together — just the weight of stone upon stone.

"Now, years ago, the farmers who built these walls maybe would have furrowed the land and used that stone as their raw materials to build the walls. The beauty of the stone wall is that they are more or less maintenance-free. Once you have them built, you don't have to do anything else to them. Like this farmer did on the right here, you can also make an opening wherever you like when you want the animals to come from one field to the other. Or, if he wants them to stay in one patch, he closes off the opening. He wouldn't consider buying a gate. He'll just throw brush and sticks across the opening where he wants them. I say that the walls are more or less maintenance-free, because you don't have to paint them and they don't rust. Now, from time to time, animals, particularly horses, like to scratch their necks on the stone walls and they might knock down a few stones, but you just come along and pick them up again. The walls along the roadside mostly have cement in them, but the ones down in the fields are the old-fashioned dry stone walls, mostly limestone. If you look closely, you can actually see daylight between the stones. That enables the strong winds to go through them instead of knocking them down.

"Oughterard means 'a place of the high view,' even though the town itself is situated down in a little dip, down at the foot of this hill.

"Just before we get into the town, here on the right, are some of the old country cottages with the thatched roofs and there's another one on the left as we round the corner. People are buying these old cottages and doing them up. That is exactly what is happening with this one, too. It has a new roof, windows, and doors.

"There is a nice hotel here — the Connemara Gateway Hotel on the left.

"This town is one of the premier angling towns in Ireland, so there are a lot of small hotels and guesthouses waiting for the fishermen when they come. You won't get a bed in this town during the month of May, when all of the fishermen will be here.

"Just over on the right is the local sports field where we play our national games in Ireland: football and hurling. For those who do not know, Gaelic football is played with a round ball, has 15 players on each team, and you can catch the ball with your hands. Hurling is like Gaelic football, but is played with a stick called a 'hurley.' A hurley is made from ash timber. The hurling ball is called a 'sliotar,' a small ball about the size of a tennis ball but made of leather. It is the fastest field game in the world, and the ball can travel at speeds of up to 100 miles per hour. Our other national sport is handball. This is now an international game and can be played indoors or outdoors with two or four players.

"None of our national sports have professional status in Ireland. The players all play as non-professionals and receive no payment for their efforts. They receive their uniforms, traveling expenses, and their meals. They play for the love of the sport. Some of our other sports like rugby, soccer and basketball are professional, but not our national sports.

"Oughterard is the second largest town in Connemara and has a population of about 2,000 people. Clifden is the largest. They are both called towns, not villages. Oughterard has only two streets in it — Main Street and Camp Street. You wouldn't get lost here. The little thatched-roof pub on the right is Power's Bar, and this is the square — the main part of the town.

"That's the Boat's Inn over there, a restaurant and bar, and also the Lake Hotel over here."

As we drove through the town on Main Street, Hugh slowed the forward motion of the bus. It was not an easy task to slow it down and still keep it moving. He pointed out the building on the left where his grandparents ran Ferguson's Grocery and Pub. It was easy to share in Hugh's pride just by the way he tilted his head and told us this is where his mother was born. His grandfather was born down on Camp Street, last house at the very bottom on the right-hand side.

"Oh! More photos of the bus — everybody smile.

"There are two churches: the Church of Ireland is on the left, the Protestant church. The family grave of the Martins of Ross is in the grounds of that church. Straight ahead is the Catholic Church at the top of the town.

"This stream here on your left is called the 'Owenriff River,' and in English it means the 'Sulphur River.' It flows into the Corrib River. During the fishing season, which starts in February and runs into September, the salmon come up the river, against the current, to spawn. These salmon travel thousands of miles to get to this river to spawn. Four years

We stood on a steel bridge above the churning water of the Owenriff River, watching salmon fighting their valiant battle to get upstream before the water becomes too shallow.

ago, they were born in this river and they come back to the river where they were born. How they know to do this is a mystery, but they do come back to spawn in the same place where they were hatched.

"The main time for the season is the month of June. We always have floods in early June, so the salmon wait for the flood and come up the river — quite a lot of them together. They lay their eggs on the sandy bottom of the river, then die. The young come down in December to go back to the sea. Then, in four years they come back and repeat the cycle.

"During the season, there are quite a number of them coming up the river, and we have seen some of them this week, jumping at the waterfall.

"I can tell by the suds on the river that there is still quite a bit of water in the river.

"You may wonder about the color of the water. As the river passes down through the peat bogs, it picks up its color, so you will notice that the water is brown in color. When it is sudsy, like today, it looks kind of like Guinness."

Hugh brought our bus up an incline and stopped. He told us that we were going to walk down to the waterfall walkway that spans the Owenriff River.

I caught a glimpse of a young boy who appeared to be about 11 or 12 years of age, standing on the back side of a stone column that may have been built as a gatepost or maybe to impede the wanderings of large animals or small vehicles. My interest was piqued because this lad was acting very much as if he had been posted there as a lookout.

My mind flashed back to the Saturday afternoon movie house, and up went my guard telling me that I should be preparing for an ambush the likes of which Gene Autry and Roy Rogers often had to be on the lookout for.

The bus rolled to a halt and the boy took off like his

gears had been greased. Hugh laughed and told us, "There are lads up ahead who have skipped school to catch their share of the salmon that are going upstream."

We stepped down from the bus and waited for Hugh to lead the way. As he was closing up the bus, he paused to point out that on one side of his bus door it says "Welcome Aboard" in English, and on the opposite side of the door is written in Irish, "Failte Isteach," meaning "Welcome Inside."

"Now, when they built this bus," Hugh explained, "there were no locks installed on it, because they weren't needed. Just a minute and I'll show you the lock." He climbed back aboard the bus and showed us an appropriate length of a one-by-two board he was preparing to slip inside the runner of the door. He emerged through the small door beside the steering wheel and said, "My lock is also handy just in case I should ever need it for something more serious."

We worked our way through the inside of tall stone walls that sheltered the pebble lane down to the steps that led to the river's edge. Sure enough, there were three boys bustling about, trying to sack several wriggling salmon into a canvas bag. When they spotted us, they tried to hurry even more, causing them to be even more clumsy. They were gathering the rest of their gear in a rush to scurry out of sight.

Hugh said, "They are looking to see if the bailiff is walking in with us. Sometimes he is." When they saw that the bailiff was not with us, they stopped what they were doing and continued fishing.

I asked how Hugh knew that this is what we would find here, and he replied, "Because I used to do it meself." He went on to explain that, "The next stop for these lads will be one of the local Bed and Breakfasts where the guests will dine on fresh salmon this evening. When local hotels and the B&Bs advertise 'fresh salmon,' it's just that."

I asked if these boys were demonstrating the true meaning of the term "poached salmon," and Hugh jumped to their defense to point out that it is not illegal to catch the salmon going upstream. "The only rule these boys are breaking today is skipping school. Then," he added, "they will do their best to get home around the time they would normally arrive home from school, so they won't also have to commit the sin of lying." His accurate description of their activities dispelled anyone's doubts that Hugh had truly done just as he claimed.

Hugh said, "These salmon will be going against the current, so you will look on the left-hand side in amongst those big rocks. Here, I'll show you where to look," he said, pointing. "We might see some and we mightn't."

We watched quietly and stood right above the churning water, on the small, but sturdy steel bridge, and here we saw the last of these champions struggling to make those final four miles upstream.

Mesmerized by the constant force of the water that was trying to keep them from reaching their destination, I felt a strong empathy as I watched them fight their valiant battle. I admired their courage, for they acted as if they knew that they were fighting such a small window of opportunity. The time frame for them to reach their goal ended this month. We were not short on sightings of the beautiful specimen. Most of us remained quiet and stood motionless, leaning over the railing, watching them struggle to fulfill their destiny. I could readily identify with them. At least they knew their destiny. I was yet to find mine.

I overheard Tom from Michigan tell Niece Number One that his battle had been almost this great, and he was sorry it took him so long to come home again. He looked at his niece and smiled. He leaned forward even farther and shared

It was in amongst the trees at the top of these steps, by the Owenriff River, where I came to terms with the death of my father.

his smile with me.

I held out my hand to his niece and said, "Would you like me to take your picture?" She handed her camera to me, then put her arm around her uncle. I moved up the stairs on the far side of the river to get a better shot of them and still include the cascading water behind. Tom from Michigan invited Lily from London to come to his other side, so I moved up one more step. Then Niece Number Two joined in and I moved up still one more step and sat down.

I said, "With this many people in such an important family photo, I probably should take two pictures just in case someone blinks at the wrong time." There were lots of hugs, but they finally released their grip on each other. They came together once more and pulled me into their group hug.

I returned the camera to Niece Number One, and we all fell silent again. We lined up along the steel railing to watch for more salmon struggling in the raging water under us.

I watched an enormous salmon make its journey all the way up the big boulders and tried to burn this into my memory, to be used for the next time I needed to draw on a resource other than my own for my next insurmountable struggle. I watched the salmon repeatedly dip into the depths of all that was inside of it to muster just a little more courage and a little more stamina, then jump again.

We had watched so many beautiful fish soar up and over the rocks in their constant battle against the river's current that it would make even a deeply religious fisherman consider trading his soul for a dip net. My daddy would probably have left the tour at this point and tried to horse-trade one of those kids out of his fishing pole. He loved to fish.

I pulled away from the group and walked to the far side of the bridge, back up the stairs that led to the unexplored portion of the riverbank. When I reached the top, I was gripped with a haunting need to touch the ground from where my roots had sprouted.

I stooped down, broke off blades of grass and rubbed them against my cheek, feeling their softness that was enhanced by the earlier rain shower. I placed the grass against my mouth and could feel my breathing passage thicken as a rush began to well up in my throat. There was absolutely nothing I could do to stop it. Nor did I try. I walked on a little farther as tears splashed down my cheeks.

My daddy always made perfect sense to me. We shared a mutual respect that made me want to be just like him in as many ways as possible. So, it was no surprise that I had been expelled from school several times before I entered high school, and every blessed time was for the same reason — fighting. I never found anyone the least bit interested in knowing that I was simply righting some of life's little wrongs like my daddy had taught me. I found out the hard way that this whole form of logic just didn't work very well for a kid — much less a girl kid.

This proved itself for the first time while we were living in St. Paul, Minnesota, where Daddy had been hired to oversee the construction of defense plants. We didn't know anyone in the area where we were living, and there were no children in our apartment building, so I was pretty much left to my own devices to make my way in this brand-new world.

Mother enrolled me in elementary school, and with no peers to guide me, I figured that things would run in Minnesota pretty much as they had in Missouri, but this turned out not to be the case. Up north, they appeared to be more sensitive — and brittle. They broke a lot easier up there. Maybe because it's so cold.

I didn't think there would be stitches involved, but I had already told this goofy kid three times to stop. I couldn't give him much more warning than to tell him three times.

Daddy told us kids only one time to do — or not to do — something, then he would pop us. If we hadn't heard him tell us, that wasn't his fault. He would say that we should have been listening.

I say that Daddy told "us," but it was only the boys he told. I only received one whipping from Daddy in my whole life. And it didn't come my way until the following year when I turned 12 years old. I was told to be home by 9 p.m., and I didn't get home until 9:40. Daddy took me upstairs and removed his razor strap from the hook where it hung in the bathroom. We stood looking at each other while he explained the importance of following rules and doing what I was told. He turned me around and gave me two lashes across the back of my thighs. The pain was not enough to make me cry, and I didn't until he put his arms around me and held me close. Then, we both cried.

Unlike Jeff, I only erred once to learn my lesson. I sent the first warning, "Jeff, stop throwing at my head." But as soon as he could, he packed another snowball good and hard, just as if he hadn't heard me at all. I had no intention of sending him to the hospital, but I did intend to stop him from throwing snowballs at my head — and I did that.

Inside the school, the principal looked at me like I was a rotting side of beef — one that had already begun to stink — hanging from a meat hook. The playground monitor had me hanging from my coat collar, which she yanked up so high and so tight that I felt fortunate to receive each new gasp of air in my lungs. The principal was pressing a damp cloth to Jeff's mouth to catch the blood, and she screwed her face up in a little bow knot and asked me, "What on earth did you do to Jeffrey to make his mouth bleed so badly?"

"I made him stop throwing snowballs at my head."

She insisted on a better answer. It looked pretty obvious

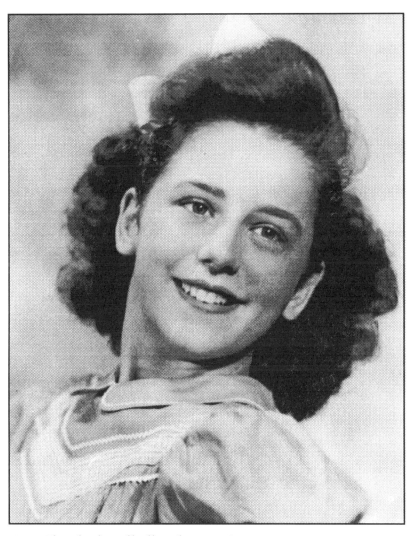

Ann Elizabeth Milholland, age 12

to me what I had done, but I explained it to her anyway, figuring her to be a little dense. I tried to use my most ladylike manner when I told her, "I distracted him with a fake right, then busted him with a left-handed uppercut and I guess he must have bitten himself in the lip."

From the look she gave me, I don't think that explanation was what she had been searching for.

The principal had already summoned the school nurse, and we all waited while she rushed in and took the blubbering, bleeding Jeffrey away, announcing that he would probably need some stitches. The principal sat down at her desk. I watched her write the note, which she tightly sealed in an envelope so I couldn't see what it said — like I didn't already have a fair idea.

The principal said, "Here. I want you to take this home to your father and tell him that you are not welcome back in this school until he brings you back to talk with me about your behavior."

I knew better than to sass anyone with authority. That included my parents, anyone else's parents, policemen, principals, teachers, neighbors, and older people of any stripe, but I was dying to tell her that it was not my behavior that had caused this, it was Jeffrey's.

I said nothing.

I figured that my daddy would be so proud when I told him how I had taken care of my own problem — the very same way he would have handled it.

What I hadn't figured on was Mom standing in the doorway wanting to know why I was home so early in the afternoon and intercepting the letter. I had been so busy rehearsing my own speech and hearing Daddy's proud reply in my head that I hadn't prepared a speech for Mom. She sat down, ripped open the envelope, read the note from the principal, looked me square in the eyes and gave me that wearisome warning, "Just you wait till your father gets home."

Up to now, I had been counting on that being a positive experience.

Mom always followed that timeworn threat by being the first to greet Daddy as he came through the door. She hadn't bothered to ask me what happened, so I figured she knew from the note. It was a tense afternoon, because if any of us kids couldn't be in school when school was in session, there was no room for any form of entertainment at home except books. Schoolbooks, not comic books. Not even library books, if they were fiction.

That evening, she met Daddy at the door and said, "Here's the outcome of teaching your hot temper to your daughter." She jammed the letter into the same hand that also held his scarred metal, lunch bucket. The same black lunch bucket that for many years harbored a cookie or part of a jelly sandwich he saved for me to find when I emptied it and wiped it out with a damp cloth.

All of a sudden I didn't feel quite so confident about whose court Daddy was going to be in for the outcome of this set.

Maybe he couldn't show how proud he was of me in front of Mom. Then, he gave me a sidelong glance and a slight jerk of his head. My heart began to sink as I followed him into the kitchen.

It was like someone geared him down to slow motion. He walked to the kitchen, with me a respectable distance behind him. I watched him place his lunch bucket on the table, slowly remove his hat, the one with the furry earflaps that tied up on top, and placed it on a chair. He laid down his dirty-palmed leather gloves, the ones that always looked like his hands were in them, whether they were or not. He took off his red-and-black plaid Mackinaw that always smelled of wood smoke, and hung it on the back of the same chair.

Daddy sat down on another kitchen chair and pulled me up on his lap so he could hear me better, then he asked me to tell him my side of what happened before he read the letter. It was the hug that told me everything was going to be all right.

Daddy was late going to work the next morning. He and I both stood and listened to the principal's outrage in describing this ruffian's behavior. When she was finished, Daddy asked her, "Would I be standing here, listening to this, if my daughter were my son?"

The principal excused me to go to my class. Daddy kissed my hand — the one he was still holding from our walk into the building. He said, "I'll see you tonight, Pal." As I gently closed the door, I looked back through the window and I could see that their horse race was a long way from the finish line.

Boys are so goofy. Later, the girl who sat behind me in class told me that I should never have hurt Jeffrey like I did, because he had a crush on me and he was only throwing snowballs at me to get my attention.

Well, forget that! He was the only person I ever knew who blew his nose on the ground during recess without the use of a handkerchief. Had I felt a wave of generosity instead of a need for justice, I guess I could have given him a handkerchief instead of stitches in his fat lip. Nah! Justice was crying to be served.

We moved back to Missouri before Daddy lost another half-day of work on my behalf.

There were a few rounds while I was still in junior high school — or middle school, as they now call it. Probably the worst one happened during physical education class. I told my teacher that it was the wrong time of the month for me to go swimming. We still needed to suit up whether we went into the water or not. She must have doubted my excuse for some reason, but, she did not follow standard procedure, which was to send me to the nurse's office for a check. Instead she positioned herself so that I had to walk on the poolside to pass by her to line up for roll call. As I did this, she told me I needed to overcome my fear of water and pushed me into the deep end of the pool.

All of my 13 years did cartwheels through my mind. I accepted it as an undisputed fact that I was an out-and-out goner, headed straight for the ocean floor. I was about to become shark bait.

Much to my surprise and maybe even to the surprise of a few others, I floundered around and finally made my way back to the edge of the pool, as my classmates watched with horror. I clung to the tiny, cold, blue-and-white square tiles that formed the overflow rim as I sputtered and coughed up no less than two or three gallons of chlorinated water, or so it seemed, trying to clear my lungs and desperately gasping to catch my next normal breath.

I waited to regain some degree of control over my trembling limbs. I don't remember, but I am sure I must have cocked my left eyebrow just a little, as my focus on breathing soon gave way to formulating my plan for dispensing a reasonable measure of justice.

I cut no slack whatsoever for the fact that Miss P.E. Teacher was wearing an expensively tailored, wool tweed suit; exquisitely complemented by a flowered, silk blouse; nylon hosiery with no obvious snags in them; and genuine alligator, medium-heeled shoes. She styled her hair to complete the Veronica Lake look, letting her hair fall over her right eye. I was only guessing that she had a right eye under all of that hair.

I heaved the upper half of my body up on the tile

walkway that surrounded the pool. After a short rest, I dragged the rest of my body out of the water, and raised myself to a wobbly standing position. Without a word, I staggered behind her and, as accurately as I could, I aimed her straight for the exact area I just vacated. I remember nodding my affirmation as I watched her score a bull's-eye — clipboard, whistle and all.

I didn't receive a total measure of satisfaction when I saw that she already knew how to swim. Even staggering under the weight of her woolen suit, she was able to make a much more graceful exit than mine. For one thing, she swam over and used the steps. But I did feel that a full measure of justice had been served.

With instructions from no one, I sensed that I should be concentrating on getting out of there. I headed for the locker room to change into my street clothes, because I knew there would be some explaining to do to someone.

The loud click startled me, but without even trying the door handle, I knew I was imprisoned in that locker room. Half-dressed, I climbed atop a row of a dozen, attached, gunmetal gray lockers and tried the ground-level windows until I found one that had not been painted shut for at least a hundred years. I climbed out into the courtyard, ran inside through the back door of the main hallway, and headed for the principal's office, hastily trying to button my blouse before my arrival.

I don't think I ever once failed to make Daddy proud of me. He never acted as if it was a chore for him to take off from work long enough to get me reinstated in school if he thought I was justified in my actions — and he always did.

I look back on this man and his daughter and wonder if Daddy might not be a little disappointed to find that today's Irish are no longer portrayed as drinkers and fighters, but instead as gentle, caring people. He probably wouldn't mind, because beneath the huff and gruff of his exterior, Daddy was also a gentle and caring person.

When I grew older, I learned better ways of handling life's little injustices. Had I not, I probably would never have been able to serve as the administrator of a graduate school or sit on the governing board of a state university. I think these positions also would have made my daddy proud, knowing that by marching me back up the front steps of every school that discharged me out the back door eventually had produced some positive rewards. Maybe these were not more significant than personally administering justice, but they were still rewards.

I knew that my paternal grandfather's ancestors, the Milhollands, came to America from Northern Ireland, and I think Daddy would understand that Ireland still has a few trouble spots flaring up here and there. He must be lookin' down and knowin' that I likewise have me own trouble spots that still flare up now and again — but not like they use to, a'tall, a'tall.

I broke off new blades of grass and began to weave a criss-cross pattern with them. After I emptied my well of tears, I made my way back onto the pebble pathway that led to the steps down to the waterfall bridge, only to see Hugh approaching the steps on the other side, searching for his missing passenger. I then realized how detached I had been, and who knew for how long? I had been alone with my daddy in his beloved Ireland — his homeland.

How could I feel so alone while surrounded by a busload of people? In the past several months, I had frequently been unable to really connect with those around me — those who go on living, breathing, so vital and alive.

Blessings are only available to those who open their hearts enough to receive them. Perhaps I had been looking for a renewal of my life with my eyes instead of my heart.

If I was a victim of my own doing, I needed to strive to be that strong person that Daddy molded after his own image. He would want me to be that person again. I had to go on living — really living.

On the distant bank of the Owenriff River, the fog that continued to enshroud me began to lift and my spirituality stirred within me. I realized that my spirit could not survive without me and I had not been a conscious contributor to its well-being for quite some time.

I think Daddy would want me to focus on the white smoke in my life, that same white smoke that is the unswerving constant of a turf fire — a fire which can beckon, lure, and magically warm the heart and soul of any lost Irish man or woman.

I brushed away the dampness from my cheeks, and walked down the steps on my side of the river, and made my way back across the bridge. I apologized to Hugh for disappearing.

He could see that I was struggling and asked if I was okay. I told him that I was moving in that direction. I just needed a little more time.

chapter seven

I WAS COMPLETELY DRAINED, as if the important muscles in my body had lost their ability to contract. Only the bumpy rhythm of the bus was keeping me awake — much against my will. I needed an escape and sleep felt like my only recourse, but my backpack made a lumpy pillow.

I barely heard Hugh telling us, "This time of the year, you can see the purple heather all in bloom, along the top of the bog. Over on the left-hand side you have the Scotch pine forest.

"Over the years, the Forestry Board has been planting pine trees, which would not be indigenous to Connemara, and now with conservation, they have decided that when these forests mature, they are going to replace the pine with broad-leaved trees like mountain ash, beech, birch and oak. They will be more common to Ireland.

"You will see mountains at the top of this hill. These mountains are part of the MaamTurk Mountains. Around the corner, we will see the Twelve Pins in the distance. The mountaintops are covered with clouds, but you can at least see part of them.

"We will be stopping shortly at The Quiet Man Bridge. It was used in the film, *The Quiet Man*, which was made here in Connemara in 1951, and directed by John Ford. Some of the main stars were John Wayne, Maureen O'Hara, Victor McLaglen, Ward Bond and Barry Fitzgerald."

As our bus began to slow down, gauze wrappings were crawling all over me — across my neck, down between my shoulder blades, inching right up behind my ears. My first thought was that I had dozed off and was dreaming. The voice I heard sounded so distant. I sat up and my eyes focused — it was Hugh's voice explaining that we had arrived at Leam, which was only one of the sites where scenes from the movie, *The Quiet Man,* had been shot.

Is this the movie I had been dreaming about? I have seen this movie twice. In my mind's eye, I could still see the scene near the beginning of the film where Barry Fitzgerald drove his horse and trap down the lane and over this very bridge, leaving a cloud of dust behind, just as our bus was doing now.

Hugh told us that we were now in the village of Leam and this bridge was originally called the Leam Bridge, but since the movie had become such a classic the local folks renamed it The Quiet Man Bridge.

Hugh stopped the bus on the crown of the bridge. I looked out my window and could actually feel the cool creek water rippling across my bare feet, and yet, I felt like I was high above or maybe somewhere else, watching all of this happen.

Hugh said, "Mary and Tom live down here by The Quiet Man Bridge. One day, in the middle of winter, Mary heard a car arriving and she wondered, 'Who is visiting us now?' She was inquisitive, so she came out of the house and saw a red car parked down by the foot of the bridge here. There were two ladies standing out of the car. She walked over to them and started telling them about the bridge and that it was used in the movie, *The Quiet Man.*

"One of the ladies asked of her, 'Have you ever seen any of the stars in the movie?' Mary said, 'No. No, I haven't. But one of them had red hair — like yours.'

Leam Bridge was built between 1850 and 1895. After it appeared in the movie, The Quiet Man, *starring John Wayne and Maureen O'Hara, the local people changed its name to The Quiet Man Bridge.*

"She said to Mary, 'Do you not recognize me?'

"Mary stood back and looked at her and said, 'No, I don't. Are you a relation of mine from America?'

"The lady replied, 'No, I am Maureen O'Hara and I was in that movie.'

"She introduced Mary to her friend and said they came to visit the bridge.

"Mary said, 'My goodness, you had better come in and have a cup of tea.'

"And so she brought them into her house. I don't know if they had a cup of tea or not, but I always say they did, for it makes a better story.

"This happened 22 years ago. Maureen O'Hara is still alive, of course. She is now in her 80s and comes to Ireland quite often.

"Now, they selected different parts of the area to make this movie. Most of the film was made around the village of Cong, which is on the northern shores of Lough Corrib, but this bridge was used in the film.

"For many, many years, my grandfather drove his bus out from the town of Oughterard to this little bridge and he would bring the people of Leam into town to church — into Oughterard. He did that every Sunday morning for 25 or 26 years, I am not exactly sure. He provided another very important service by bringing people to church on Sunday morning. I remember coming out here with him as well, going down to this little bridge and collecting these people for church."

Hugh seemed to drift away from us sometimes, as if he were remembering some other grand time he'd had with his grandfather, or maybe something he chose not to share with us. He told his stories as if this was the first time he had shared his memories with anyone. It made sense that it wasn't, but he made me feel that way.

"I came down here one day last week and found that someone had run into this end of the bridge, here on the left. They ran into it with their car and knocked it down. The stones had fallen into the water below. I didn't want my passengers to see it in that condition, so a friend who was with me helped me rebuild this end of the bridge. We retrieved the stones from below and did a job that was not too bad, as you can see. It looks much better than it did. And it seems to be holding up."

Hugh finished driving across the bridge and said, "The sign out on the roadway tells of The Quiet Man Bridge and also the Connemara Cottages. Those are the little cottages up on the hillside there.

"This is a quiet, peaceful little village here. Sometimes you get some of the small tour buses coming down in here, but not many."

As Hugh had done several times already, he made us feel like a very privileged group. And we were.

"On the right-hand side here, this cream-colored building was the schoolhouse at one time. See the plaque on the building that says, 'Leam National School, built in 1877.' There were about 20 students and one teacher. It is not a school anymore. If we wait around here until half six on any Saturday evening, the local priest from up at Oughterard comes and says Mass. It is now used as a church.

"A couple of weeks ago, I drove the bus down here and Mary was walking down the lane with a man named John, I think his name was, John somebody from Massachusetts. His ancestors lived in Tom and Mary's house before emigrating to America during the famine. He was the first one of his entire family to visit Ireland again.

"When he found that the school his family had attended had been turned into a church, he went straight away to town and bought a marble-topped table for the priest to use for his sacraments, to replace the wooden box he had been using.

"John also brought along an oil painting with him that one of his aunts had painted and he presented it to Mary. It was the picture of bog workers stopping to pray the Angelus, at 6:00 in the evening.

"John and Mary were just walking back down the lane from placing the table and hanging the picture in the church when we arrived. On that particular bus trip, there were four people on board from Massachusetts who lived quite near to John's home.

"If Mary is home, she will open the church and show you what John presented to the church.

"I have to turn the bus around here. I can't go up this road, because the small byroad is too narrow for the bus.

"There are blackberries right there on the side of the road, if anyone is interested in having a taste.

"This house right where we are turning around here was the gatekeeper's house for the railroad. The Great Midland West Railway Company traveled through Connemara at one time, from Galway to Clifden. And it would have come through this field here. See the embankments? And see those two pillars there on the roadside? They were actually part of the railway crossing. This little cottage was one of the railway cottages. The company was set up in 1895 and it closed down in 1935. You can see on this shed, the lintel on the doorway is one of the railway sleepers. It was a steam train that traveled from Galway to Clifden for 40 years."

Hugh pulled forward and parked, and we all stepped down from the bus. We were very careful walking among our feathered greeters. Hugh said, "Here, we have chickens and ducks as well, you see? I come here to buy eggs from Mary's free-range chickens."

The lintel over the doorway came from one of the railway sleepers (railroad ties) from the Great Midland West Railway Company. The steam train traveled through Connemara from 1895 till 1935.

He called to Tom from Michigan that this was the chicken and duck stop. Tom from Michigan laughed, along with everyone else.

"Danny the Donkey and his offspring associate the bus with eating. So, you can feed him, but be careful, because Danny bites. A lady from New Zealand received a bad bite from Danny just this summer, and I had to dress her finger for her. She said she'll be telling all of the people back home that she was bitten by Danny the Donkey in Connemara, Ireland."

Hugh continued talking about the bridge, "It was originally built as a dry bridge, maybe 150 years ago. Once it became famous, the traffic increased, and souvenir seekers started to carry off pieces of the stone, so it has now been cemented in order to help preserve it."

I observed the cement between the stones and wondered why we humans continue to satisfy our hunger for material things, when so many of us are actually experiencing the need to feed our souls?

I walked away from the bus and the bridge. I walked up the lane and looked over the stone fence and knew immediately that I had found "my field." It did not even resemble the one I had envisioned in my mind earlier that morning, for this one was even more picturesque — more perfect. The rolling green hills tumbled down toward me as I walked away from the sounds of the water gently rippling over limestone boulders orchestrating the serenity enfolding me.

The gravel crunched beneath my feet. Walking alone was my way of putting distance between me and my own reality. I listened to the gentleness of the quiet. I was walking back through the centuries to another time. I was lost in a state of meditation, as the taut strings inside of me began to unwind and release the burdens and sorrow of my past.

From the gravel lane at The Quiet Man Bridge, I looked over the stone fence and knew I had found my perfect field.

I was allowing the sounds of the water from the stream to cleanse me, for there were no more tears left inside me.

I tried to ignore the footsteps behind me, and I did not turn. It was Ted from England who joined me. We exchanged glances, but not words. I did not want his company, but once he caught up with me, he kept in step as we walked. I stopped and fondled every wildflower I heard call my name, whether I recognized it by name or not. Ted watched my every move. We walked on to see what was beyond the twists and turns and found the donkeys standing near a small rock house. I wondered which was Danny and which was his offspring. They were confined by only a short, rock fence and returned our gaze with a look of welcome.

I was beginning to experience the feeling of renewal I had been seeking, not as a visitor, but as a true Irish lass. I was walking heart-in-heart with some of my ancestors and could feel the warmth of their presence. I was completely engulfed in an emotional peacefulness and knew I had truly come home.

The young man looked at me and offered me a half-smile. We walked into the heart of this tiny community where I could see only signs of life, or past life, but no people. This is precisely where I belonged — or perhaps I had belonged here in the past.

Hugh walked toward us in the lane and, as he approached, we both stopped and turned. Instead of closing the gap between us, he gave a wave of his hand — kind of a half-salute, as if telling us to continue with our mission. He walked back toward the bus and the other passengers.

I was experiencing a kind of bittersweet victory since I had agreed to fight rather than yield to defeat. It was like turning a corner that I didn't ever want to even peek around — never again, because I now felt that there was a Higher Power who had not released me from my duties yet. I needed to continue my struggle to find my new purpose in my life — to work until I reached my destiny, whatever it may be and wherever it may lie.

I also understood that I could not continue to live my life in the shadows of the ones who had gone before me and still expect sunshine to wrap its arms around me and bring me in out of my darkness.

For me, a form of renewal is walking in the woods, anticipating the loneliness of slipping into the comfort of boughs that meet overhead; a shaded avenue, the Irish call it in English. In Irish it is called a boreen. It allows me to escape from the harshness of my world. I sometimes dread emerging back into the sunlight, for instead of my hopes for regeneration, the harshness too often delineates my hollow-eyed world of realism.

This time, I gathered my recent sorrows, those that remained of my husband, my father, my great-grandfather, and tried to tuck them into a flaming blossom on the fuchsia growing beside me, but decided its delicate blooms were too tiny. So I mentally scattered them on the pebble pathway at the foot of the thriving bush, then counted them where they fell. I only hoped they were all present and accounted for. If not, the forgotten ones would have to wait. I turned and walked away.

As Ted and I neared the bus, I was drawn to the fading blossoms of the peppermint plant and decided that my dealings with death itself needed to accompany the passing of this fragrant plant. They could join together and bloom again in another time as fresh new blooms within the inner recesses of renewed life.

A lightness of spirit began to embrace me.

Hugh told us it was time to leave. I was not ready to move on. I was fighting a desire to stay right here in Leam where I had escaped from the pain of my todays, ready to make an even exchange for the hardships of yesterdays, but I knew that like his grandfather, Hugh would never go off and leave me.

Ted from England and I emerged from the lane, quietly immersed in our own thoughts, and I expected the closure within me to bring about something profound, but instead, Ruthie rushed up and asked me to take a picture of her standing beside the bridge.

I looked through the camera lens at this beautiful, young, lone traveler and pictured her hiking this road 60 years ago. I could see Andrew screeching his old bus to a halt and offering a free ride to this hiker with the Australian flag stuck in her rucksack. He would have liked her and admired her spirit of life and adventure.

As we walked back to the bus, Ted turned and offered me the other half of his only smile.

I glanced back at the beautiful spot where I had left my burdens. I had visited The Quiet Man Bridge and the village of Leam with a quiet young man.

chapter eight

HUGH TOLD THOSE who wanted to take pictures to walk across the bridge and he would drive the bus up to the crest and stop for them. This pleased everyone with a camera. The others crossed over with them to be out of their pictures.

I found Dennis talking with Ted from Michigan. I patted him on the arm and told him I was going to move back in the bus and try to rest.

"Are you okay, Sis?"

"I will be. I just need to rest for a while."

He started to follow and I asked him not to. I climbed aboard, collected my backpack from my seat and moved to the long seat across the back of the bus.

Hugh climbed aboard and pulled up on the bridge for the picture-taking session, and I nestled down in the back corner by the window.

I was still reluctant to leave The Quiet Man Bridge and the solemn little townland of Leam, but I smiled when I thought of the part of me that remained back on that gravel lane. I could still smell the fragrance of the wildflowers. It was in Leam that I planted my heart in the soil of my heritage, and would wait for it to bloom again. It would happen in another time, but in the perfect place.

When the photo opportunity had ended, Hugh finished driving across the bridge and collected his passengers.

Pete from New Jersey walked back to his seat and looked at me but didn't sit down. I finally looked up at him and he asked, "Are you okay?"

"I am getting that way."

Pete smiled at me and sat down again behind Drew. I listened to them visit until Hugh started to talk again.

I sat back up as Hugh shifted the bus down into first gear. We growled our way up the hill that would return us to the roadway, and Hugh told about the small children who frequently sit in the front seat beside him. "I always ask them to help push the bus to get it back up this steep hill. The little ones will lean on the dash and push and grunt. Last week, a little red-haired boy from Northern Ireland worked up a real sweat pushing the bus up this hill."

Today, the bus struggled on its own to get the job done, for Ruthie didn't take the hint.

"Another nice lake view on the left-hand side. It is believed that a hermit monk did live there at one time and that's how it got the name, 'Hermit Island.'

"You will see that the sheep there along the roadside have markings on them. The markings are mainly for identification purposes. Several farmers might rent the same section of land, and they paint the backs of their sheep blue, red or green — or combinations of those colors if there are more than three farmers — to identify which sheep are theirs.

Connemara is more suitable for sheep farming than for cattle, because the land is so poor. At one time there were subsidies given for raising sheep, and now they are trying to discourage farmers from raising them. The numbers of sheep are so great, the farmers are being forced to practically give them away. They have overgrazed the mountains, and it is time now to control them. The number of sheep allowed will depend on the number of acres a farmer owns.

"Look at the roadway over on the other side of this

lake, you can still see where the railroad line used to run. The train would have traveled on the far side of this lake, called Bofin Lake. Over that 50-mile journey, if you traveled by train in those days, there were seven stops for the train and four times as many bridges — 28 bridges. Lots of water in Ireland.

"The next stop for the train would have been Maam Cross and that is where we are going to have our stop today as well. And this is where we will be turning around and heading back toward Galway.

"On a Saturday, there still is a mart here at Maam Cross. For many, many years, there used to be a Fair Day here at Maam Cross, where the farmers would meet and sell their stock: horses, sheep and some cattle. People from all around the area used to gather here years ago on Fair Day.

"Now, there is a bar and a restaurant and a craft shop, and a replica of The Quiet Man cottage. It has almost life-sized wax figures of the four main characters of the movie. I say almost, because John Wayne is not quite as tall as he really was, and Victor is not as heavy as he was. I was told that they made John Wayne shorter because of the low ceiling in the cottage. I am not sure why they trimmed Victor down.

Hugh stood to reset the hands of the clock and told everyone to notice the time, because we would be leaving in 30 minutes from this time. He said, "If you are not back on the bus, we can wait on you for a little while, but not long.

"I lost a German fellow one time. He started walking, went up to the corner, turned left, and when time came to leave, we waited about 15 minutes. I walked up to see if I could find him and I couldn't, so we left without him. That was about two years ago and I haven't seen him since. So, if anyone sees him, tell him that he still has a return trip coming to him."

Lily asked if Hugh had ever lost anyone else on the trip and he replied, "Only in the bog. I turned to talk to another gentleman and when I turned back, the first one was gone. There he was down in the bog. He had fallen in. But we fished him out and finished the tour.

"Now, we'll go inside, have a cup of tea — or something stronger, if you like, and we will meet back here in 30 minutes."

I did not go with the others. Dennis was visiting with Tom from Michigan and I told him I was going to walk up to the crossing and see if I could find what lured the German fellow to abandon the trip. Ted from England, the quiet young man, walked with me. About 25 yards up the road we left the roadway and climbed a slight incline and shared a large rock for a seat.

The heather was clutching its lavender blooms and, in spite of the balmy weather, was releasing its hold on the greenery and allowing it to rust, but it was still beautiful.

I looked around this little cove in the lake and appreciated the beauty of the gnarly trees, which were barely holding their grip to the side of the bank, and the shrubs, which were still flourishing. I wished I could live in that little white cottage over there with the slate roof and red brick chimney.

Someone had tucked their boat up under one of the trees, with perfect assurance that it would be safe until their return to use it again. I reflected on the magnificent beauty of this beloved country and gave a little prayer of thanks for the healing it had afforded me.

Perhaps the German fellow also had meditated here on this rock and decided that he needed to walk on up to the next crossroad and see what was in store for him there.

I settled into a comfortable sense of synergy that was

My meditation spot. I wished I could live in that little white cottage over there with the slate roof and red brick chimney.

beginning to fit me well. I promised myself that I would visit this very spot again someday, for it would remind me of the day I managed to align my spirit and my emotions in perfect harmony. I would call this my meditation spot, to give thanks for the beginning of the search for the remainder of my destiny. I didn't know what that destiny would be, but I knew when I started my search for it.

I was not alone in leaving a part of myself back in that lane in Leam, for the young man who joined me there also joined me here to meditate. Ted opened his heart to me as we rested on our rock. He told me his reason for being on this tour.

Ted started talking with frequent hesitations, saying, "I have been watching you and I feel as if you are going through much the same things that I am."

"And what would that be, Ted?"

"I am not sure, but I doubt if you are an orphan, like I am."

"Yes, as a matter of fact, I am an orphan, but in my case that is a natural progression since I am probably older than your parents."

"I can't address that. You see, I am 34 years old and have lived my entire life in London as an Englishman. It was only six weeks ago that I buried both of my parents as the result of a devastating auto accident."

I expressed my condolences.

Ted dropped his head, and I placed my hand on his shoulder. When he gained control of his emotions again, he said, "Being their only child, it fell on me to settle their estate. In doing this, I had the burdensome duty of sorting through their papers, trying to understand and deal with the different facets of their lives. We never discussed what would happen at the time of their deaths, for they were relatively young people.

"I was searching to see if they had even drawn a will when I discovered," he stopped talking and sat quietly for a long while, "my adoption papers. I learned for the first time that I had been born to a young unwed Irish girl."

Again he struggled for control, but his voice broke. He turned his head away to study the water in the lake.

He was finally able to continue, "I am visiting Connemara, trying to disentangle the lie that I have lived my entire life."

"I yearn for just a feel of my birth mother's presence, and in doing so, I have been introducing my English self to my Irish roots — in search of a feeling of closeness to a woman I never knew. And will never know. I learned only yesterday that she, too, died earlier this year."

Ted flatly stated, "No one in this world could ever feel more alone than I feel right now."

What was left of my heart went out to him as we sat and studied the lake, trying to absorb more of our serene surroundings.

chapter nine

WE CLIMBED ABOARD the bus for our return trip to Galway. Hugh counted noses and determined that we were all present and accounted for. He slid into the driver's seat, turned on his microphone and steered the bus back onto the roadway.

Hugh looked in his rearview mirror and told us, "Next, we are going to stop at a famine village. This particular one is called Lettercraff."

I caught my breath, much like the Irish do here on the west coast. Was I ready to revisit Lettercraff after I had just dealt with so many other emotions today? I felt like I had allowed everything to surface and be recognized, and now I wasn't sure what would pop up next to nip me. I guess I would find out.

"There are quite a few of these deserted villages around," Hugh continued. "They date back to the potato famine during 1845 to 1849, when so many people were reliant on the potato. Many villages were evacuated during those years. Once the potato got the blight and the people had nothing to eat, they were forced to move away from their villages. This is actually what happened to this little village.

"We cannot go into the village because, first of all, it is quite a long way from the main road, but I will stop and we can look in. I will try to show you where some of the houses were when this village was inhabited.

"I have a photo album that I will pass around showing the remains of some of the houses in the village. You will see that some of the land was also used for growing vegetables as well as potatoes. In the photographs, you will see what we call the lazy beds. These are the ridges where the potatoes were grown.

"The village itself is on this hillside. You can see the stone walls up there. The green fields were at one time part of the land of the people who lived in this village. The green fields indicate the area where most of the houses were situated.

"As I said, this deserted village was called Lettercraff. Before the famine there were 13 families living there. The reason it is located so far up on the hillside is because the old road to Clifden ran right below them at one time, long before this present road was built. The road we are on was built about 90 years ago."

Hugh pulled over to the side of the road, stopped the bus, and stood so he could direct our attention.

"Look over to the left-hand side. See the field up in the left-hand corner? Do you see the wide wall? That was actually one of the houses. Down from that field is another mound of stones. That is the remains of another house.

"The families deserted their homes in 1846, because of the blight to the potato crop. They had no choice. Though there are no crosses, this is considered to be sacred ground. The remains of these villages are considered to be a memorial to the millions who lost their lives during that time.

"Some of the families who lived here were the Geaghans, Molloys, Darcys, and O'Tooles. They didn't all emigrate, for some of them moved into the town of Oughterard and some of their descendants live there still. Others did emigrate, mostly to America.

"These were bleak years in the west of Ireland. There

were feeding stations that started in August of 1846 which fed 10,000 people in one day from what was called a 'famine pot.' It was a metal pot big enough for a man to sit in. It was about four to five feet deep and three feet wide.

"Before the famine, the population of Ireland was around eight million people. Two million emigrated and close to two million died. Ireland has never regained its original population. The population of Ireland today is in the area of four million, maybe a little more."

Hugh's words were vying for my attention. My mind kept slipping back to the previous afternoon, which had been a day of introduction, introspection and interconnection during my visit to this village. I was intently striving to connect with Hugh's words. He was looking out the bus window and pointing up the same mountain I had climbed only 24 hours before.

He held my attention for a while, saying, "One of my friends from the Old Galway Society, an archaeologist and historian, came on this tour with me a while back," he said. "When I pointed out this village of Lettercraff, as I am doing for you now, my friend told me he had never heard of it before. This is because there are so many of these little famine villages all around our countryside.

"He asked me to take him up to Lettercraff someday. I haven't done that yet, but I intend to do it soon. He will be able to show me things that are staring me in the face, things that I have been unable to recognize, things he will see right away as an archaeologist."

As Hugh continued to describe the village, I kept slipping away from his words to again relive portions of my own journey on this seemingly barren hillside.

I was again pulled back by Hugh's words and the fact that I saw the other passengers beginning to step down to the roadside. I joined them both physically and mentally.

The wind was blowing my hair and my eyes were stinging. I searched the top of the mountain for my Connemara ponies, but there were no signs of them.

Lily from England, quoted a poem she remembered from when she lived in Ireland. It was written by M. J. MacManus, in 1849:

"A plague-wind blew across the land,
Fever was in the air,
Fields were black that once were green
And death was everywhere."

Hugh broke the silence, which had overtaken the entire group by adding, "With no warning, four million people already upon the verge of destitution were deprived of their staple food, and half of them died."

I had to walk away. I could taste the warm saltiness of my own blood and slackened my jaw to release the biting grip on the inside of my cheek. I looked to the top of the mountain again in search of my Connemara ponies, but they were not there.

I was again struck by the wondrous occurrence that had taken place on this sacred ground only yesterday. My Connemara ponies had snuggled in as tightly as they dared to nudge, close enough to share in a moment that will forever be a part of me. I think it must have been my profound experience with them that regenerated my soul enough to breathe life into my new sense of belonging. I had no choice but to give them credit for nurturing my resolutions today at the Owenriff River and again at The Quiet Man Bridge. It may have been God who sent the new awareness to my heart, but it was the messengers that I still visualized in my mind's eye.

chapter ten

"THERE ARE THE FARMERS bringing home the turf," Hugh pointed out. "We have experienced a very wet summer, and even though it is wet, the turf will dry — eventually. The farmer has been much more concerned about bringing in his hay, because if it was to get wet, it would be ruined. There is some of the dry turf being brought home now.

"For many, many generations here in Ireland, people have cut the turf into rectangles, we call them sods — a sod of turf, or peat — and we burn peat in the fire. The tradition is still with us, where people cut the turf the old-fashioned way, using the sláne. Some will employ somebody with a machine to cut the turf. All over Ireland we have a certain amount of bog land. It is not just unique to Connemara. We are approaching some of the peat bogs here in Connemara. Most of this land here on the left side consists of peat bogs. See the families down there cutting?

"The rain washes down these granite mountains into the lakes and into the bogs.

"Some commercial farmers cut the turf using machinery rather than cutting by hand. This one is commercial — Keogh's Bogs, it is called.

"Many families now have central heating, but still enjoy an open peat fire. They might buy peat for about a pound a bag instead of cutting it. Of course, if you prefer to cut your own, you can rent a bog and pay by the yard.

"I have a sláne in the boot of the bus. I will show it to you when we stop so you can see what it looks like. I have a basket of dry turf, as well."

In 1930, H.V. Morton wrote *In Search of Ireland*, "I hear men and women of Connemara singing in the fields. Sounds go a long way in this still country, I hear the click of spade against stones and a voice lifted in some old Gaelic song. I would give anything to understand it. I have never wished to understand a foreign tongue so much."

Me, too.

When we arrived at the Bogs of Maam, Hugh took us only to the edge of the bog, because he said it was too wet to enter.

Hugh got into the boot of the bus and showed us the dried peat and his sláne. The peat dried hard and was un-believably heavy. He said, "All of the moisture is dried from it, because it is from last year's turf. And this is called a breast sláne. You cut from the breast instead of under your foot."

The sláne looked like an L-shaped spade, with a sharp-ened straight edge all along the cutting sides. Hugh empha-sized that it must be kept very sharp at all times.

He demonstrated how it is used, and explained, "Nor-mally, the cutting of peat begins around St. Patrick's Day and is cut through the rest of March, April and May. It is brought out of the bogs and stacked along the roadside during June, July and August to dry. It is turned over and stacked in reeks [ricks] to continue drying and is then pre-sented for sale. It is either removed by the buyer, or by the cutter for his own home use, during September, October, and November. Peat is still the main source of fuel for some Connemara homes."

Mona from California asked, "What keeps people from stealing the peat stacked along the roadside?"

A local Oughterard man "bringing home the turf" during the 1920s.

Peat (or turf) is stacked alongside the roadway during June, July and August to dry. Peat is still the main source of heat in some homes in Ireland.

This was a perfectly obvious question for an American from a large city to ask.

Hugh gave her a wide-eyed look of astonishment and said, "In Ireland, you may very well steal a man's money, but no one would ever steal another man's peat.

"A lorry-load costs about £400 [$600] delivered to the door," Hugh told us. "The average user burns £300 to £400 worth per year. You always store one year in advance to allow for thorough drying and more efficient burning. When you build a house, you set aside space for the turf shed. To many, the turf shed is an important part of living, an important part of surviving. Whole families will work together to get the peat in before the onset of winter.

"Turf cutters can usually work down about 20 feet before striking rock. There may be several owners to one area of bog land. You must obtain permission to cut even one piece of sod from any of the bog lands. I previously obtained permission from this owner to show you how to cut the turf, even though I don't intend to carry it away."

He told us about some pretty amazing things that have been found while cutting peat. A golden chalice, estimated to be worth £25 million, was found and is now on display at the National Museum in Dublin. The body of a Viking warrior believed to be 5,000 years old was found and is on display in Denmark.

Hugh scuffed his toe to uncover some of the richest soil I have ever seen. He exposed a quality of peat that would cost us a dear price at home.

At the precise moment when he told us about how spongy the earth under the roadway was, a truck rumbled by us. We actually felt the asphalt move beneath our feet, kind of like a surfer catching a wave. Hugh watched us become wide-eyed, then he laughed and told us the roadway must be repaired almost annually due to the lack of a

The rains wash down the granite mountains, then into the lakes and the peat bogs.

solid foundation.

I have lived a long time, but that is the first time I ever actually felt the earth move beneath my feet.

Mabel, Mona and Kevin from California must surely have been thinking "Earthquake!"

chapter eleven

"HERE WE ARE back in the little town of Oughterard again," Hugh said. "This time, we will drive down to the pier on the shore of Lough Corrib. But first, let's take this road that goes off to the left here opposite the gate to the Owenriff River. This is part of the Old Road to Clifden before the present road was built."

Hugh pulled onto the Old Road to Clifden and stopped, then asked if anyone knew what building you would find when first entering a town or village in the olden days. No one spoke up. He pointed to a building that still had what looked like a lay-by alongside which could have accommodated a team of horses. The side of the building could have been a shed before it was enclosed.

"Years ago, the blacksmith was one of the most important people in town. He wasn't there just to shoe the horses. He provided many services for the people of the community, and one of them might have been making up cures for people.

"In fact, my father-in-law, Dennis Stack, was a blacksmith down in County Cork. In addition to his regular blacksmith duties, Denny used to make up an ointment or a cream, made of milk and poitín, which was a kind of home brew, and he would rub it on people's muscles. He had a cure in his hands. It was a combination of his hands and the ointment. People came to him from all around for all kinds of treatments."

One of the passengers who boarded the bus at Salthill, an Israeli man who now hailed from Kenya, interrupted Hugh and said that he and his family once lived in Roundstone.

"As a child, my brother fell and broke one of his permanent teeth while playing. He was in great pain, so with no dentist in town, my father took him to the blacksmith to have his tooth pulled."

I wondered how this man happened to travel from a few miles down the road here in Connemara all the way to Kenya and back, but I didn't interrupt Hugh to find out.

"The blacksmith would always make up a supply of slánes for people to buy for the new peat cutting season ahead.

"As you would expect, you enter the village of Oughterard on this old road, and this first premises was the blacksmith's. As the old carriages were coming through, people might be in need of having their horses re-shod or they might need a fresh team of horses.

"The day came when the blacksmith was not quite as busy, but still just as important. My brother Liam says that when he was a youngster of about six or seven years of age, he would spend all of his afternoons under the shed of Paddy Tom Joe, our local blacksmith, watching him at his work. Liam said that one day a hot spark came off the horseshoe while Paddy Tom Joe was hitting it with the hammer atop the anvil. The hot spark went under the strap of Liam's sandal and he roared with pain. Liam says what a holler he gave up! Paddy Tom Joe picked him up and stuck him feet first down in a wooden barrel of water. Liam says he can still smell his flesh smoldering to this very day. He now carries a mark as big as a half crown on his foot. He talks about how he spent many, many happy days under the blacksmith's shed with Paddy Tom Joe.

"Another friend of ours, Paddy O'Halloran, says that Paddy Tom Joe was also a watchman for the mothers in the neighborhood. When the youngsters would try to work their way up toward Main Street, Paddy Tom Joe would boom out in a big voice and ask where they thought they were going, and all of the children would scoot back toward their own yards again. They never gave up trying to get past him, but they could seldom manage it. The mothers felt quite secure that their children were being watched while they went about their chores.

"So you see, there were many reasons why the blacksmith was such an important person in the community."

I didn't hear the remainder of what Hugh said, for I looked across the road and saw the stone gatepost where the young lad had been standing as "lookout" for the salmon poachers on our way toward Maam Cross.

Now, on our return trip from Maam Cross, I realized what a great distance my emotions had traveled since I dealt with my daddy on the bank of the Owenriff River earlier in the afternoon.

I felt as if both of my feet had been firmly planted on the ground — Irish ground — and my heart was not carrying such a heavy burden.

chapter twelve

HUGH TOLD US that our last stop was to be the pier at Lough Corrib. From the main road, he turned onto a "shaded avenue" barely wide enough to keep the tree limbs from scratching the sides of his bus.

"As I have told you, this area relies heavily on the fishermen who come down to Lough Corrib during the month of May trying to catch mainly the wild brown trout and the salmon.

"Lough Corrib is the largest freshwater lake in the Republic of Ireland and provides the drinking water for the city of Galway. From the pier, we will be able see a few of its islands. Some are occupied and have houses on them. One island contains a working farm and a Victorian house on it. It was just recently listed for sale, then sold for an enormous price.

"There are wonderful brown trout in this lake just waiting to be caught. Mayflies cover the lake and lay their eggs. The eggs then drop to the bottom for incubation. When they hatch and rise to float on top of the lake, the local boys gather the flies from the shores of the lake and the surrounding bushes and sell them to fishermen for £1 per dozen. My nephew made as much as £40 per day last spring, which was quite a different pay scale from when I was a youngster gathering mayflies.

"You have to watch rather closely when the young lads

are counting out their mayflies. Sometimes, the lads are a little slow in releasing them. The mayflies might travel between his box and yours several times before it is actually deposited. The boys continue counting as that same fly goes back and forth a few times."

After a moderate pause, Hugh looked at us in the rearview mirror and said, "I guess they still do that." The corners of his eyes were crinkling again.

"There goes a boat that brings people out on cruises on the lake. Corrib Cruises, it is called."

Hugh tipped the left side of the bus down toward the edge of the water on the boat ramp and asked Ruthie if she could swim. No one heard her answer, but into the microphone, Hugh said, "Oh! Too bad!" It felt exactly like we were going to roll over into the water. He backed the bus up to the opposite edge of the lane and parked it, explaining that if he didn't do that now, we would have a hard time getting out later if more vehicles were to arrive.

Everyone walked out on the pier and staked out a little territory of their own, almost as if they wanted to soak up as much of this beauty as possible.

Drew walked up beside me and asked, "Where are you from in Missouri?"

"I usually say I am from Kansas City, but actually, I am from Independence. They are two separate cities, but we share an invisible dividing line and are both part of the same metropolitan area."

I don't think it was my answer that was the conversation stopper, but the tranquility of our surroundings.

After a while I turned my face into the wind and looked toward Drew, "How long are you here for?"

"This is my third week of six months."

"In Ireland?" I asked with envy.

"No, in Europe."

"Mike, too?"

"No, Mike is leaving to return home tomorrow morning."

We fell back quiet again.

Probably five minutes passed as we stood there basking in the glory of this lake and County Mayo on the opposite shores.

"I have been watching you trying to connect with Pia from Switzerland. Are you making any progress?"

Drew said, "Not yet. I have been trying to get something going for tonight, but she has plans with two of the girls she's traveling with, so it doesn't look promising."

"Don't give up. Six months, minus three weeks, gives you time, if not here, maybe somewhere else."

Drew shot me a grin and ambled over toward Pia. The last time I looked, he was writing something on a scrap of paper.

Hugh began to talk and we all flocked to him much like a bunch of baby chicks gathering around a bowl of grain.

"This big island with the big tall trees, straight ahead of us, is called Innishanbo. It has a lovely Victorian house on the other side of the island — we can't see it from here. It belongs to a businessman from County Cork. He bought the island, along with five other islands as well for £2.25 million just recently. He is in the computer business. The Connemara area seems to attract computer people for some reason.

"My grandfather used to collect his cargo from this pier and then deliver it to merchants throughout Connemara who contracted for his delivery services. Andrew knew where his services were needed, and he went out of his way to make life easier for as many people as possible."

Everyone fell quiet again, except for those who visited in hushed voices. I hardly ever visit Missouri's Lake of the

Ozarks for more than an occasional weekend. I am sure the serenity of Lough Corrib must be what many of the people there once knew and would prefer now, instead of the jet-skis, water skiers behind speedboats, cove parties, boat-hopping, and general hell-raising that have caused the water patrol to double and triple their numbers.

I was beginning to believe that Hugh was intuitive enough to read the minds of his passengers. He walked by and said, "Small fishing boats are about the only types of boats seen on this lake."

He stopped by Drew, Pia, Mike, and Pete to show the general direction of points of interest across the lake, in case they had the opportunity to go to the other side of the lake.

As we climbed aboard the Connemara Bus to depart Lough Corrib, there was a noticeable stillness among the passengers. Was it the turn of the beautiful fall day to a cloudy evening that was causing the change of mood? Maybe a little melancholia, or perhaps fatigue?

Hugh had displayed unquestionable expertise in the way he had melted away all of the barriers we strangers managed to create for ourselves. His undeniable skills had manipulated this busload of strangers into a busload of new friends, representing America from the Atlantic to the Pacific, Australia, Germany, Kenya, Japan, England, Switzerland, and other parts of Ireland.

The brief friendships that were formed also caused Hugh problems as he struggled most of the afternoon to keep us corralled and on schedule, but he never lost his patience, his gentle nature, or his smile. Now, collectively, we were showing signs of some degree of closure, like coming to the last ten pages of an outstanding book. We didn't want it to end.

Our bus was growling at us again as Hugh pulled away

from the pier. He drove beneath the boughs of the trees that met overhead, and said, "What I didn't show you earlier were the lights on the bus. I will turn them on going through this shaded avenue here, so you can get an idea of what the bus looks like in the nighttime. Pretty romantic, isn't it? It makes a lovely glow."

This completed our visit to the past. It was easy to imagine Andrew delivering the weary women back to their little townlands in Connemara, and everyone chattering about the things that had happened during their day at Saturday's market in Galway.

Hugh paused before pulling back onto Highway N59, which would carry us back to Galway. He would not let our beautiful afternoon end on a downturned or a sad note, so he put a tape in the recorder. He explained which parts we were expected to sing and where we were to clap our hands. Before he started the tape, he told us about two little girls who sat beside him in the front seat several weeks ago.

"I asked these two little girls to keep watch for those on the bus who didn't sing. If they spotted someone not singing, they were to tell me straight away and I would pull right over and put them off of the bus."

He said, "The little girl closest to me, Elizabeth, kept peeking around the edge of the seat. When the song was finished, I asked her if everyone sang. She looked at me with her eyes quite wide and quickly replied, 'Yes, they did. They surely did.' She was so afraid that I was going to put someone off the bus."

Hugh put the tape in the recording machine, but something was keeping the tape from engaging tightly enough to produce music. It kept cutting out.

The quiet little Japanese girl, who had been sitting in the seat right ahead of Dennis, had not uttered a word since she told us her name early in the day. Thinking she didn't speak English, no one had tried to seek her out. All of us were so wrong.

By experimenting, she found that by holding her foot in just the right spot on one corner of the tape, she allowed us to launch right into our assigned musical parts.

In less than a mile, Hugh had elevated our spirits back up to the level they had been most of the afternoon. We were all trying to respond to just the right part of Din Joe's recording of — what else?

THE CONNEMARA BUS

It passes each day down the village street
    Is there any chance of a vacant seat?
There might be now — take the weight off your feet
    On the Connemara bus.

You'll get to Galway what 'ere befalls,
    Driving along by the low stone walls;
The women all wearing their bright woolly shawls
    On the Connemara bus.

The journey would surely be worth your while;
    The yarns and Gaelic would make you smile;
The women discussing the latest style
    On the Connemara bus.

Now baskets of eggs will be pearched on the rack,
    You'll hear the ducks as they quack, quack, quack,
Their yellow beaks sticking out of the sack
    On the Connemara bus.

You would certainly know it was market day,
    The chickens cheerping all the way.
We talk about prices as we sway
    On the Connemara bus.

To the city of Galway it goes once a week;
    It's a great excursion so to speak,
With laughing women all rosy of cheek
    On the Connemara bus.

To all newcomers we smile and we nod;
    Be careful there of that fishing rod
It's a grand soft day, so thanks be to God
    For the Connemara bus.

Hugh led the singing and sang along with us. Each place we were to clap our hands, he would raise his left thumb in the air.

When we finished singing "The Connemara Bus," he tooted the horn several times and we all applauded.

Thanks to quiet little Lee from Japan and the long stretch of her right leg, we were entertained with Irish fiddle, bohdrán drums, uilleann pipes and tin whistle, all played in an upbeat tempo that carried us right along with it. We teased Lee from Japan that it was only fair, since the Japanese had taken over the electronic technology for the world, that she be the one to rescue us.

"Hey, I like to do my part for all mankind," she replied.

The voices around me were harmonizing and singing the lively Irish ballads that followed. Some voices were beautiful and some were not beautiful. Even in the ballads that followed, most of us instinctively knew where to clap our hands. Some of the ladies wearing leather heels were tapping them in unison to make clogging sounds along with certain songs. It sounded like the Connemara Bus version of "Riverdance."

When the music finished, we applauded our musical talents again, and Hugh led a second round of applause for Lee from Japan. She stood up and took a bow. We learned about the real Lee from Japan much too late in the day.

By the time we returned to Galway, almost an hour behind schedule, no one had escaped the sharing, fun, laughter, or the application of our limited musical skills.

A larger bus, or a driver who lived elsewhere, never could have given us the insight into the heart of Connemara as Hugh had done. He is an integrated thread in the fabric of the countryside and he weaves intricate designs for you to wrap around yourself while his words stroke your spirit with gentleness.

We were all exhausted and hungry, but our delayed evening meal would have to wait a little longer as we exchanged addresses, then bid each other farewell and safe journey.

We may all return to different parts of the world, but each of us will forever hold the beauty of Connemara in our hearts, along with our warm, new friendship with Hugh Ryan.

Hugh told us that on the few occasions when there are empty seats on the old green bus, a quiet little lady slips into one, never paying a fare. This frequent rider to Maam Cross and back to Galway city sits alone near the back of the bus and seldom enters into the festivities. Neither he nor Liam seek her out or divulge her identity to any of the other passengers, for their mother, Freda, does not want to be a part of their presentation. She wants to observe and enjoy. If only for a four-hour period, she wants to recapture a significant part of her past.

Instead of finding my own family, I found peace, serenity, a renewed spirit, and a heart full of gratitude.

chapter thirteen

DENNIS AND I GOT OFF the Connemara Bus at Salthill instead of riding back to the Eyre Square with Hugh. We had bid our farewells, and were walking without talking as we made our way back to the townhouse.

We were crossing a street when I stopped right in the middle and announced, "I am going to write a book about Andrew Ferguson!"

Dennis' simple reply was, "Go for it, Sis, but let's get to the other side of the street to finish discussing it." He took hold of my elbow and steered me safely across the street.

Fully aware that Dennis is the writer in the family, I asked, "Will you help me?"

His reply, was, "No, but I will give you all of the encouragement you need."

I sat down that evening and started writing an outline of the story and questions I needed to have answered. I had to wait four days before I found the courage to step back onto the bus again and say, "Hugh, I took your tour last Friday, and …"

Hugh said, "Actually, it was last Thursday."

Incredible!

I finally found my voice again and said, "I was wondering if you would be opposed to me writing either a story or a book about you and your grandfather."

He invited me to come up into the bus and take a seat.

I sat one seat ahead of him and across the aisle. My voice was quavering and my cold hands were shaking.

I felt obliged to tell Hugh about myself, but the more I talked, the faster I talked, and the less sense I made. "I have never written a book before, even though I was in the throes of writing my first young adult fiction novel when my husband died last January, but when he died, my whole life stopped, including my writing and ...."

If he had wanted to say something, I was not giving him the opportunity. I continued to list my lack of qualifications and finally I was making no sense whatsoever.

Hugh listened to me, but his face was missing that warm smile that caused his eyes to crinkle. He appeared to be carefully evaluating my proposal, but was very reluctant to agree to anything — and who could blame him, the way I was babbling?

I finally stopped jabbering long enough for him to get a word in edgeways, and he said, "I think it would be better if you talked to my brother, Liam. As I told you on the tour, Liam was the conductor for much longer than I was. He worked with our grandfather for almost 10 years."

I was still tripping over my words, but managed to say, "Then, you wouldn't object if I wrote about the bus?"

His reply was, "You and I can talk again, after you talk to Liam. He will be here tomorrow. You come up around noon and talk with him, and see what he thinks about it."

I thanked him and left.

How foolish of me to think he would be flattered by my proposal. I took the long way back to the townhouse, crossing over Wolf Tone Bridge and choosing the pathway along the river. The swans rushed over to me thinking I might have something to feed them. I stopped and showed them my empty hands and confided in them, saying, "I wish I had not even come to town today. You should have warned

The swans on the Corrib River swam over to me thinking I might have something to feed them. I showed them my empty hands and they turned away.

me that I was going to make a fool of myself."

The next morning, I walked back to Eyre Square and found someone sitting on the Connemara Bus who wasn't Hugh, so I assumed it was Liam. I knocked lightly on the door of the bus and asked, "Are you Liam Ryan?"

He answered, "Indeed I am."

Liam welcomed me aboard the bus, and I introduced myself. I could tell just by looking that Hugh and Liam were brothers, but Liam's demeanor still had that mischievous streak of a small boy's fun-loving ways about him. His smile was even more infectious than Hugh's, which I didn't think was possible. I repeated what I had told Hugh, only this time it was in a more organized fashion.

"Do you have a problem with my wanting to write a book about your grandfather?"

"Not at all. Here, have a seat and we'll talk."

The Irish have such a warm way of saying "not at all." It is with an inflection that makes it sound like "not a'tall."

I sat down across the aisle and one seat ahead of him and started asking questions from the list I had been compiling since I finished the tour on Friday — no, Thursday evening.

Liam was so easy to talk to. You could tell he dearly loved talking about his grandfather as much as Hugh. Tears would well up in his eyes as I listened to him relate his experiences.

I wished I had been smart enough to bring my tape recorder. Further proof of my naivete.

I met with Liam for three more mornings, and my notebook was swelling with notes. Sometimes I had a little trouble with Liam's Irish accent, but from across the aisle, he was watching my notes closely, correcting them when the need arose.

One of the first questions I asked of him was, "What

was the exact name of your grandfather's place of business?"

He replied, "It was Fairguson's Bear."

I wrote Fairguson's Bear and he said, "No, it is 'Fairguson's Bear.'"

I wrote it again, this time as "Ferguson's Bear.'"

He smiled at me and flicked his finger at the page in my notebook and said, "That's it. Now, just knock that 'e' up out of the bear and you'll have it."

I wrote "Ferguson's Bar," and he gave me a big grin and said, "There you are!"

After the first session I had few problems, unless, of course, he said something in Irish, which he was always careful to translate.

My writing about the Connemara Bus turned out to be like my own genealogy efforts, the more I learned about the Ferguson story, the more I wanted to know.

Hugh's warm personality returned in a flash. He and his wife, Debbie, invited me to have dinner in their home, so I could meet their children: Paul, Deborah, Gillian and Andrew. When I arrived, I glanced into the living room, and there was my blazing turf fire. Again, I was beginning to feel as if I had come home.

I had a hard time engaging my dinner partner, Andrew, age seven, in conversation. I finally decided that he must have been cautioned about talking too much at the dinner table, so he whispered all of his responses.

After dinner, the adults retired to the living room with glasses of wine and settled in before the turf fire. Hugh insisted I take the chair right beside the fireplace — the place of honor.

I said, "Hugh, before I let you read anything I have written, I need to know why you were so hesitant when I came to the bus and asked your permission to write about Andrew?"

His reply was, "You are not the first one to ask permission to write about the bus, but apparently you are the first one who is going to follow through with it."

"Yes, I am going to follow through with it, but I can't do it on my own. I need to know more facts and more stories. I need specific incidents."

"You'll get them. In fact, now that I know you are serious, I have set up some meetings for you."

"Meetings?"

"Yes. They are not definite arrangements yet, but I will let you know when they are. Did you bring something for us to read?"

"I have, but you will see how stilted my writing is because I have no real feeling for Andrew and Daisy. I had to fabricate the scenario at the beginning with the facts I had, and this is not what I want to do with the story. I want real stories about them."

I handed a couple of sheets of paper to Debbie and asked if she would read the beginning of the story. She agreed and read aloud:

Andrew eased his weary body down on a park bench to read his letter again.

12 March 1920

My Dearest Andrew:

Since your father died, I have tried, but find that I am unable to cope with the demands of the business.

Your sister, Julia, has been helping me, as have others, but I think you should make preparations to return home.

I feel the proper thing to do at this time is to turn the business over to you, the eldest son.

Your loving mother,
Deborah Ferguson

Andrew stared at each word of the letter, nodding to it before moving to the next. When he finished reading his mother's name for the third time, he refolded the paper and slipped it back into the envelope, lowered his gaze and sat quietly. His beloved Daisy sat beside him ready to share his burden.

She broke the silence with "Andrew?" He passed the letter to her, and she read it without comment. She looked down at his hand still resting on the park bench. She slid her hand inside his, and he acknowledged her presence with a gentle squeeze. They sat watching the Yangtze River pass by. The water offered a sense of calm that they both needed at this moment.

"My parents grew old while I was off living my life," Andrew told her. "I was so busy doing my part with the British Army when my father died, I was unable to help my mother in any way. I guess I just took it for granted that everything was running smoothly — with my brothers there to help her. I can't believe it has been 15 years since I left home. I came here as such a young lad, and I will be returning to Ireland as a man."

Andrew turned and asked, "Will you be going to Ireland with me, as my wife, Daisy?"

"Yes, Andrew, I will, now that you have asked."

He was careful not to squeeze her tiny little hand too hard, for the sizes of their hands were so mismatched — unlike their love. Their smiles displayed such tender understanding that even a casual observer would have been able to see the depth of their feelings for each other.

"Tell me about your parents, Andrew." Daisy already knew about his parents, but her nurse's training led her to believe that it would be good for Andrew to talk about his home right at that moment. It would help him untie any knots of guilt that might be holding his heart captive.

Andrew told her that he knew very little about his parents' early days together, other than that his mother, Deborah Breen, was born in Cahersiveen in County Kerry and his father, Hugh Ferguson, was born in Ballinamore in County Leitrim. His father, a sergeant in the Royal Irish Constabulary, had met his mother while stationed in Kerry. Together, they had provided him with a comfortable home and a childhood as good as any of his friends, but he didn't know much more than that to tell her.

"One thing I know for sure is that I must return home to help my mother before I lose her, too. She needs me."

Andrew's focus returned to the river. Daisy watched his face as his gaze would affix to something moving along with the current, then move quickly back upstream to repeat the journey with the next floating object he found. She turned her gaze to the river, too, and sat quietly, allowing Andrew to sort through the remainder of his thoughts.

When he first came to China in 1905, Andrew served as Chinese Corps commandant with the Shanghai Police Force, working his way to the rank of sergeant. At the outbreak of the world war, he volunteered to serve in the British Army, eventually becoming a captain. His first battle was in Kiochow, followed by serving in China, Malaysia, Singapore, Mesopotamia, Kenya and Tanganyika. His army days ended in the marshaling yards of Canada before returning to Shanghai and his work with the police force.

After some time had passed, Daisy drew Andrew's thoughts back to her by saying, "Tell me about the family business and what I will be doing when we arrive there."

Andrew smiled at her again and said, "The family business is officially called Ferguson's Bar, but it is a grocery on one side and a pub on the other. This is a very common combination in the villages and towns of Ireland. You may hear it referred to only as Ferguson's or Ferguson's Grocery or Ferguson's Pub. It is located on the west coast of Ireland, in the town of Oughterard in a region called Connemara. If there is such a thing as the most beautiful part of Ireland, it is, indeed, where you will find your new home."

Andrew's thoughts began to wander again. "There have been so many signs pointing toward a bright future for me right here in Shanghai," he said. "I guess I had taken it for granted that I would spend out my days right here with you."

Daisy reached to touch Andrew's face and said, "If this turn in our pathway hadn't appeared, you might never have gotten around to asking me to marry you, Andrew."

He turned to receive her sweet smile and kissed the palm of her hand that rested so gently on his cheek.

Hugh and Debbie said that all of the facts I had incorporated were correct, and I had captured the essence of the two of them very well, but agreed with me that we needed to tell stories that would show the compassionate people that everyone in Connemara remembered.

Hugh said he would make appointments for me to meet his mother, Freda, as well as cousins, friends, neighbors — and anyone else who had known Andrew well.

Hugh refilled our wine glasses as Debbie added more turf to the fire.

Those living in the Connemara area today are as kind and generous with visitors as they are with their very own. They are not only hardy people — they are a gentle people.

Hospitality is part of the Gaelic code and, like the Irish language, is a significant thread in their fiber — the strength of which was busy weaving a soulful design on my heart.

chapter fourteen

IRISH PUBS have their own charm. It can be something as simple as the name "Liam" carved in the rafter above my head, or the glassy-eyed gentleman making his eighth trip to the gents' room in the past 30 minutes just so he could wink at me as he walked by. Each time he walked by, Debbie would nudge my knee to bring my attention to him.

"I am sure he would be open to an introduction," Debbie whispered.

"Do you know him?"

"No, but I am quite sure he wants to know you."

"I think I'll pass, if you don't mind."

Debbie and I were trying very hard not to giggle like a couple of schoolgirls. My smile was gone as soon as my attention was drawn to the opposite side of us.

I wondered how Andrew would have treated the four-some next to us who appeared to be what I recognized as "bikers."

I didn't judge them by the Harley Davidson motorcycles outside the front door, but instead by their black leather vests they wore over their black T-shirts and sometimes just their tattooed bodies. I was surprised to see that there was no message printed on the back of the leather vest of the man next to me. I expected it to read, "If you can read this, my old lady fell off," or something equally as clever.

We had not gathered in the Mayfly Bar for its

ambiance. Instead, we were there because it was originally Ferguson's Grocery and Bar in the town of Oughterard. We were there for a brief visit into Andrew Ferguson's past through the mental images and keen words of the people who knew him best.

Andrew and Daisy's only child, Winifred Ferguson Ryan, gave no notice to the people around us. Probably Andrew wouldn't have either. I learned that he pretty much allowed people to live their own lives, but he and Daisy had a sixth sense about when to subtly provide a helping hand without being asked.

Freda sat just as she stood, with impeccable posture. First glance suggested the stature of a matriarch, but closer inspection revealed a sparkle in her eyes and a gentleness of features that reflects the love her family bestows upon her in such generous portions. She responds to "Freda," "Mammy" or "Nanny," depending on who was is addressing her.

Mammy and Da are common names for parents in Ireland. Her children's Da passed on in 1978, and it is quite apparent that she now received double portions of love from her seven children.

Freda's second son, Liam, and her third son, Hugh, were sitting with us in the bar that had belonged to her parents, Andrew and Daisy Ferguson. It was in this same bar that she had worked as a young girl. It was in the living quarters above this grocery and pub where she had been born.

Freda glanced around and said, "My, it looks so different to me now."

It seemed apparent that she was sifting and drifting back through the years of her life in this very pub. She gave no indication that her mental journey was anything but a pleasant one. We all sat quietly while she reminisced. We were waiting for her two nephews, Pat O'Halloran and Brendan

Sgt. Andrew Ferguson (right) serving in the Shanghai Police Force.

Ferguson, and two old friends, Roger Finnerty and Frank O'Toole, to join us.

Freda began to sort through the papers she had brought with her, showing pictures and identifying each person for me.

Freda's nephews arrived. Pat O'Halloran's mother was Andrew's youngest sister, Julia, and Brendan Ferguson's father was Andrew's youngest brother, Maurice.

More perfect posture. Pat and Brendan both looked like military men. As it turned out, only Pat was retired military, but Brendan's stride appeared as if he could have been also.

Once Frank O'Toole and Roger Finnerty arrived, they, along with Pat, Brendan and Frank O'Toole, took their time sizing me up. When it appeared that they decided that I might be okay, I was asked why I wanted to write a book about Andrew. It seemed to be a fair question. I explained about losing my direction in life and what had caused it, taking Hugh's Connemara Bus tour, and how the tour had inadvertently turned my life around.

The ragged truth of my answers must have been adequate, for the next question came from Brendan as he began a congenial search through my history.

Roger Finnerty's wealth of white hair and lack of wrinkles in his face made it difficult to judge his age, but I soon learned that he, along with Andrew's nephew, Henny, had filled the slot of the sons Andrew never had.

Roger's words flowed so fast when he talked about Andrew, I had a hard time following his beautiful Irish brogue as it wrapped itself around his throaty chuckles. Occasionally, his voice would settle into the stillness of a pool of water and his eyes would mist a little. I had no problems understanding his brogue when he slowed down. His voice would assume a reverential quality when he

Daisy Heal was a nurse, registered to practice in the Municipal Hospitals of Shanghai. This photo was taken just prior to her marriage to Andrew Ferguson.

BRIEF SKETCH OF
FERGUSON/RYAN FAMILIES

*Hugh Ferguson married Deborah Breen
    Children:
        Patrick .. Died young
      * Andrew First owner of Connemara Bus
        Hugh .... Moved to Australia and lived out his life
        Mary ..... Died young — Son "Henny" O'Halloran
                 was first Connemara Bus conductor
        Eugene Followed Andrew to Shanghai
        Nora ...... Followed Andrew to Shanghai
        Julia ...... Helped mother in family business —
                 Son, Pat O'Halloran, contributed
                 memories

*Andrew Ferguson married Daisy Heal
    Child: *Winifred (Freda) married
        William (Bill) Ryan
    Children:
        Cornelius First grandson to be bus conductor
        Liam .... Andrew's next and long-time
                 conductor
        Anne .... Frequent traveler on the bus
        Margaret ... Frequent traveler on the bus
      * Hugh .... Last conductor on old bus and
                 owner/driver of new Connemara
                 Bus
        Freda .... Frequent traveler on the bus
        Anthony ... Located new Connemara Bus in
                 England for Hugh

described Andrew's goodness and kindness.

Later, I was thankful that Hugh had almost total recall of the conversations when I asked him to tell me about the portions of Roger's stories I had missed.

It was the same with Frank O'Toole. Frank had such vivid recall of Andrew that he was able to transform all of us into a part of the stories he was telling — and he had a whole evening's worth. I was sorry the length of the evening hadn't allowed him to get them all told.

During the evening, Hugh kept an eye on my facial expressions, and when Frank or Roger said something so Irish that he thought I might not understand, he would repeat it back to the person talking, only in a more descriptive manner for me.

Roger asked, "Did you talk to Tim Molloy?"

"We have. We invited him to join us here this evening, but he had other plans, so we may meet with him yet another time."

It was difficult to remain an outsider in this collection of Andrew admirers for very long. It was no time at all before everyone could add a little something to the previous storyteller's version. It was easy to appreciate all facets, because Hugh had sketched his grandfather so accurately during the tour. These people were only adding the depth of color I needed to complete the dimensions of a more complete portrait of Andrew Ferguson.

Freda began the stories about Andrew. Her recollections had such a quality of richness and pride.

"As a lad of 18, my father stood on Main Street, looking in a shop window in our village of Oughterard where he read an advertisement for recruits to work with the British Army, but not as soldiers.

"Andrew made his decision to respond to the ad. He then went to London for the appropriate examinations, so the time of the preparations took him into the next year. It was 1905 before Andrew left home.

"He was sent to Shanghai. You see, on the Yangtze River, people were living on their boats, and quite a lot of barges were traveling up and down, delivering goods. There was always a lot of activity going on — and also pilfering. My father worked in the Shanghai Police Force and patrolled the river.

"It was in the course of performing these duties that found him visiting the hospital to investigate a crime or to see about someone who had been injured. It was in that hospital where my father and mother met."

Freda sorted through her papers and produced Daisy's nursing license, adding, "This is a Shanghai Medical Council Certificate of Training allowing my mother to practice in the municipal hospitals. It was issued to Daisy Heal on April 1, 1917 and was valid until April 1, 1920, signed by the Commissioner of Public Health.

"My mother was the daughter of missionaries, James and Matilda Heal," Freda said. "Daisy was born in Bedford, Lancashire, England, while her parents were home on leave. Her two sisters and five brothers were all born in Shanghai and spent most of their younger years living in China.

"Both of my parents were from large families, but I was an only child." Freda offered this and nothing more.

"My father was Hugh and Deborah Ferguson's second child, born right here in Oughterard on Camp Street. First came Patrick, who died quite young, and then came Andrew. After Andrew there was Hugh, who later moved to Australia, living out the rest of his life there. Mary, or May, as she was called, lived next door to the pub. She was a fairly young mother when she died, leaving small children. Eugene was next in line, then came Nora. They were the two who followed Andrew to China. Julia was next, and

This photo of Andrew Ferguson was taken at the time of his marriage to Daisy Heal, and is the only known evidence that he ever wore a necktie.

was the one who helped her mother try to hold the business together. Pat O'Halloran, here, is Julia's son. Last in line was Maurice, who lived across the street from the shop. Brendan, his son," she turned to point in his direction, "still lives there."

Pat O'Halloran said, "At the time Andrew answered the advertisement, the British had the run of the administration of China — such as the police and post office and that type of thing. Andrew became a member of the police force in Shanghai, which was then an international city.

"When war broke out in Europe in 1914, all of the major powers of the world were involved in it," Pat continued. "The trench systems which started at the English Channel and went on down to the Swiss border, had to be manually dug by hand. This was before the days of heavy equipment, like Hi-Macs and JCBs.

"None of the British, French, or Germans could afford to have their own men digging, because they were needed on the front lines for combat duty. So, they organized a labor force drawn from China.

"They were organized along military lines, but they were a non-combat unit and their officers were British. That is where the likes of Andrew stepped in. By this time, Andrew was speaking fluent Cantonese and was able to give the orders to the laborers in their own language, which was a big asset for all.

"Added to Andrew's immediate burdens of returning home," Pat continued, "he felt he would have more to do than just get himself home, for his brother and sister were also to be considered. As was often the case, when an older sibling left home, they would send for younger ones in the family if they found it advisable, and Andrew had done this. Once settled in Shanghai, he sent for his brother, Eugene, and sister, Nora, to come join him. Eugene found work with the customs office, and Nora became a secretary."

In the course of sorting through everything, Andrew decided that his siblings were capable of taking care of themselves, and it was Daisy that stood tall in his mind.

Actually, Daisy did not stand very tall at all, somewhere around five feet, a petite and delicate little lady. But she stood sturdy and dependable in both spirit and resolve. To Andrew, these were her most admirable traits.

Andrew had been reluctant to ask Daisy to leave her family, and live in another country with his family, for this would be a big adjustment for her. He did find the courage to ask her to be his wife, and her answer almost made him forget all of his immediate life changes and the burdens that went with them.

The wedding plans grew to such elegant proportions that Andrew recognized early on that he would probably have to wear a tie for the occasion — and he did.

Mr. and Mrs. Andrew Ferguson spent their honeymoon touring a great portion of the world on their voyage to their new home in Oughterard in the County of Galway, Ireland.

Daisy set about making her place in this Irish family by first making a good home for Andrew. She didn't do much to help Andrew with the pub side of the business, but she soon fit in nicely with his mother and sister in operating the grocery side.

It took the townspeople months to accept Daisy completely, because she looked quite different from the fair-skinned Irish lasses. She continued to just be herself and waited for the townsfolk to accept her in their own good time. She was quick to offer her nursing skills to those who needed her, and before too long she had found her place in the village by becoming a quiet but important part of many people's lives.

Andrew's nephew, Brendan Ferguson, said, "Daisy was

dark-skinned and her hair was quite long, which she wound up into a bun and pinned at the back. Some of the people who lived in the village thought her to be Chinese. You could occasionally notice people looking at her.

"I can remember when I was a young lad, I used to stay at her house with my cousins, Connie and Liam Ryan, over the shop at the old house. We would be out on summer holidays and I would stay with them then, and also on weekends.

"Daisy would prepare to go to bed at night — I can still picture her — she would have her hair kept in a bun during the day, but at night, going to bed, she would have long, flowing hair down her back. She looked Oriental to me, too, while she sat brushing her hair."

Pat related that "Andrew's brother, Eugene, did not return to Oughterard at the same time as Andrew and Daisy, but returned later. Nora married an English chap by the name of Chase and remained in Shanghai.

"The Japanese invaded China in 1932 and captured Shanghai, but left the international settlement alone — that is, until Pearl Harbor was bombed. Then, the Japanese moved in and took over the international settlement, and Nora spent time in a prisoner-of-war camp in Shanghai.

"Her husband fell ill and was released from the camp in 1945, allowing him to return to England to see his family, where he died.

"Nora never came home. She moved to Canada with her daughter, then to the United States and lived out her years there."

chapter Fifteen

WHEN ANDREW FERGUSON RETURNED to Ireland to introduce his new bride to his homeland, the country was still reeling from the political turmoil of the early 1920s. After what the Irish still refer to as "The Troubles" were brought to terms, the country was in the process of becoming a free state.

There were then and still are today only two streets in Oughterard, Main Street and Camp Street. It was a garrison town for the British Army, and at the bottom of Camp Street were the British barracks. The Royal Irish Constabulary (RIC) was the interim authority in overseeing the transition to Ireland's freedom.

The newlyweds were beginning to settle into the routine of pub and grocery merchants when Andrew's acute business sense recognized that the opportunity to purchase a surplus army truck would greatly expand the services he could offer the people of Connemara.

During these troubled times the goods from Galway could not be transported to Oughterard by road because there were still soldiers patrolling the roads, so the goods had to be brought in by boat. The Eglinton Canal was allowing cargo from the sea in Galway to be deposited directly onto the pier at Lough Corrib, and Andrew saw this as an opportunity to transport that cargo from the pier to its ultimate destination. Throughout Connemara, he contracted with merchants to deliver their goods to them.

One night, Andrew traveled down to the pier on the shores of the lake to collect his goods from one of the steamers that had come to the quay. After collecting them, he loaded up his lorry and was about to be on his way home again, when he was stopped by the RIC.

"The soldiers stopped him and accused him of smuggling guns for the old IRA," Pat O'Halloran told us. "He was made to empty his lorry and place everything out into the road. When the soldiers found they were mistaken, they simply walked away, leaving Andrew to put everything back again on his own. His youngest brother, Maurice, went to the pier to see why it was taking him so long to return and found Andrew struggling to reload the lorry — handling the load of goods for the third time that night."

Andrew knew he was taking a gamble to buy another truck, but business was thriving and his still keen foresight told him that he needed a second truck to allow further expansion of the grocery business. He took his chance and won.

Maurice drove the second truck for a while. They stowed provisions into this second truck from the grocery store and began making deliveries to the homes of friends and neighbors in nearby villages and townlands. Andrew fast became a major player in his community by enriching the daily lives of the rural Connemara people. Ferguson's Grocery and Bar was expanding onto the roadways of Connemara. Daisy, Julia and her mother continued to tend the business on Main Street.

At the same time that Andrew agreed to assume responsibility for the family business, the next-door garage went to Maurice. He traveled to Cork to learn automotive mechanics at the Ford Motor Company and kept all of

Andrew's vehicles in good running order.

The grocery and pub had a kitchen in the back and bedrooms upstairs and also served as the family's home.

Andrew's sister, May O'Halloran, mother of Joe, Jimmy, Maurice, and Henry "Henny," lived next door to the shop. Hugh remembered that May died quite young, leaving her young children on their own. Family members rallied around to help tend to the children's needs.

Hugh said, "Their house was attached to the business, you see. Henny would climb through the kitchen window and my grandmother — then, in later years, my mother, too — would feed him his meals. I was just a small lad, but I never outgrew thinking that this seemed to be an odd event, Henny climbing through the kitchen window for his dinner."

Longtime friend Roger Finnerty emphasized the kindness and interconnection of the Ferguson family and used the cows to make his point. He shook his head, smiled, and said, "They were a very close family, very close, and they had such fine cows, very fine cows. Andrew had a cow, Maurice had a cow and the O'Hallorans had a cow; three cows and they were all reared together. They would bring home the cows in turn. Then, how those cows were fed, fed to the nines. One for each house. The cows used to graze the fields out the back of Fergusons — back of the lane."

Liam said, "One of the cows was named 'Polly' and I think another one was 'Bess.' I used to go down the lane in the evening for the cows and walk them home. I also helped to milk them — all by hand, of course.

"I remember one Sunday evening when Henny was milking one of the cows. He had a lovely, brand-new white shirt on, as he was intending to go to the dance that evening. Suddenly, the cow swished her tail around and hit the bold

Henny across the face and down the new shirt. It left a lovely stripe of 'you know what' across Henny's face and down the front of the new shirt. Henny gave the bucket of milk a kick down the yard, and there was no milk to bring in that night."

Brendan, said, "When I was a young lad — and I mean a young lad — I used to bring the cows in for my grandmother, Deborah, and my reward was a small glass of Guinness. It was served to me in a whiskey glass. She was a firm believer that a small amount of Guinness was good for children. And, of course, I didn't object.

"I remember, too," Brendan continued, "that there were always two or three people drinking in the kitchen, during the daytime when we would come over for sweets. I had noticed that in all of the other pubs, people seemed to be drinking in the pub.

"One day, I innocently asked my grandmother, 'Why are these people in the kitchen?' Her reply was, 'If they think I am going to stand out there, listening to their chattering all day over two or three pints, they are badly mistaken. They can drink in here in the kitchen, where I can do me work. Then if they want another pint, I can run out for it.' They were sitting on the bench seat in the kitchen, beside the fire."

Several in the group nodded their heads in agreement. They all remembered the bench seat in the kitchen, beside the turf fire.

Brendan continued, "I remember some gents who came up from the islands on the Corrib. They were caretakers on the island called Innishanbo where there's a house built on it. It is inhabited today, but there were two caretakers working out there then and together they used to come in every so often. Well, actually, one of them used to come in every evening."

"And have a few pints," Hugh added. "They wouldn't be in the bar, they would be back in the kitchen, too — on the bench seat. I remember Daisy feeding them. She would have a pot of stew on the back of the stove. They would get a bowl of it. And Andrew would be trying to listen to the radio. Looking for the news — the world news."

"My memory of Andrew and the news was when we would be sleeping at night," Brendan said. "At what to me would be an unearthly hour of the morning — it was probably only around 12:00 or half twelve — but you would hear this loud whistling noise, and Andrew would be tuning into the BBC Home Service International News. Wouldn't Andrew have loved this satellite Sky News, where you know the news immediately?

"Your father, the Lord have mercy on the two of them," Brendan nodded toward Hugh and continued, "your father used to be on night duty when he was a Garda (policeman), and he would be attempting to go to sleep while Andrew would be attempting to tune into BBC. This was after Andrew retired, and, at that stage, I think he was beginning to lose his sense of time. He was older then. He had moved to town to live with your family. Your father got a job done on that radio, anyway. I don't remember what he did, but the reception was no longer the same after that. Andrew didn't get any more news, but your father did get some sleep."

"No one ever knew for sure how much or how little sleep my grandfather required to continue the strenuous schedule that he worked," Liam said, "because his reading lamp was hardly ever shut off during the night. He was always current on politics and world news, though."

"I don't think my father slept very much at all," said Freda. "When I was helping him make his truck deliveries, we would leave around 6 a.m. and wouldn't get back until late at night. I was just learning to drive at the time. I would travel with him in the truck, because he would get so weary. We would take turns driving.

"We didn't drive the route every day. Monday was the day we went through Connemara to deliver the commercial goods — the large quantities. We would go to Leenane, Kylemore Abbey, and on to Clifden.

"Then, the next Monday, we would go to Recess and Ballyconneely. One week we would do the north up to Clifden, and then the next week we would do the south.

"During World War II, when petrol was in such short supply, we had to shorten the run and do them both in one day. That meant an even longer day for us, starting much earlier than 6 a.m. and not returning until almost midnight.

"This is when I used to take over the driving for him. He would be so tired, he could hardly hold on to the steering wheel any longer." The weariness of fatigue was revealed in the temporary slump of Freda's shoulders as she began to reflect on those days. It was easy to read the hardships of the times in her face.

"On Tuesdays, my father would come into Galway in the lorry and collect his own goods for the shop. Tuesday was the day for bulk sugar and flour and the different needs for the animals. He would go down on the docks and get the sugar and the tea at McDonagh's. Then, he would go to the bridge mill for the flour and the bran.

"On Thursdays, we had the traveling shop for the usual household goods in smaller quantities; you know, tea, sugar, flour. In exchange, we would collect eggs and butter, for that is how they paid for their goods at that time. The people didn't have money.

"I guess we were real pioneers, because we were the only ones running at that time. We were the original traveling shop, carrying groceries and household items. This began

Freda Ferguson (left), age 12, seated beside her mother, Daisy Ferguson

in the early '30s and we were the only ones running for years.

Roger Finnerty added, "Andrew was not just a publican," which I later learned was a pub owner, "but he also had a special license to act as a wholesaler, supplying the bars in Oughterard with beer."

To the surprise of Andrew's two grandsons, Hugh and Liam, their mother confirmed this with, "Oh, yes, he did. He supplied stout to the big bars. There were big timber barrels in a place down behind the store where we used to bottle — it was the bottling shed. I got to wash the bottles, and it was a dirty, dirty job. We would put some special liquid in them, then we would wash them in a big wooden tub and rinse them. They would get two or three rinses in different water. Then, we would put them to drain.

"On another day, we would start to fill the half-pint bottles. We had a machine where you could just put the bottle on the lip and the stout would come through. There was another machine for corking. We'd leave them overnight and then stamp them. I am not sure what the stamp was for, because he had his regular license to operate, but we would put the stamp in some kind of liquid and stick it on the bottle. Then, we would have to leave them for a week or two.

"Two or three of us would be working together. There were the cousins who lived next door, the O'Hallorans; Joe, Henny and myself would all work in the bottling shed. This was when I was younger, maybe 10 to 12 years of age. Everyone helped out.

"My father would then deliver mostly to the big bars and the shops in Oughterard. He would take some of the bottles to one or two of the shops in Connemara when he delivered the commercial business, but mostly, he delivered here in Oughterard."

Frank O'Toole added, "I remember them bottling the beer; the Guinness — I do. Along with bottling the beer, they'd also cut up the butter. It came in big boxes. You'd cut up the butter in pound sizes; there were no half-pounds then. The tea came loose and that was all done up by weight. It came in big boxes, too. And then they'd do the beer. Yes, I remember all that."

The smile on Frank's face and the faraway look in his eyes told us that he had left us to live again in the pleasant memories of some of his yesteryears.

chapter sixteen

AS A VISITOR TO IRELAND — a visitor who is also a Protestant — I was completely in the dark when Andrew's family and friends began talking about him beginning the pilgrimages to Knock Shrine. I had no choice but to ask the history of the shrine.

On the rainy evening of Thursday, August 21, 1879, around 8 o'clock in the evening, a heavenly blaze of light appeared at the south gable of the Church of St. John the Baptist in Knock. In this blinding light there appeared a plain altar, and on the altar there were a cross, a lamb and angels. The Blessed Virgin Mary appeared in an attitude of prayer with her eyes and hands raised toward Heaven. On her head was a crown, and over the crown was a golden rose. St. Joseph was on her right in an attitude of respect. St. John stood on her left, wearing vestments resembling a bishop and a small mitre. He appeared to be preaching, holding an open book in his left hand. All three figures wore white.

Fifteen people, whose ages ranged from six to 75 years, witnessed this. One witness was quite a long distance from the church at the time. The group included men, women, teenagers, and children.

The rain drenched all the observers standing before the gable, but when they carefully examined the ground with their hands, they found that no rain had fallen in or around the gable. Even the gable itself was perfectly dry. The witnesses watched for over two hours while reciting the rosary.

The Most Reverend Dr. John MacHale created a commission, and after carefully examining all fifteen witnesses, the commission reported the evidence to be trustworthy and satisfactory. The report was publicized in newspapers, and pilgrims began to visit from all parts of Ireland and the world. Hundreds of cures of the sick and disabled were reported.

The first organized pilgrimage came from Limerick and was received by Archbishop MacHale. A second commission, established in 1936, re-examined the three living official witnesses, who reconfirmed the evidence they had given in 1879.

Andrew Ferguson's business activities continued to expand when he was asked to provide transportation to special events. Long-time friend Tim Molloy was the first to ask Andrew if he would be interested in taking a group to Knock Shrine on a pilgrimage. Andrew thought about it for a while and decided he could fit it into his already busy schedule.

Tim shared his photographs and stories with us, saying, "When the Pioneer Association started their outings to Knock Shrine, we had only a small group, but it wasn't long before we had to hire two buses. We always used Andrew's bus first, whenever he was available."

Andrew decided to make these trips regular events by adding benches in the back of one of his trucks.

Pat O'Halloran's father, Phil, who was a fine carpenter, retrofitted the flat bed of Andrew's second lorry by building sides and attaching wooden arches to support a canvas covering. He built a door and several steps down the back to allow some degree of comfort for the passengers.

People were a little slow in contacting Andrew about

making the trip to Knock, so he drove down to the village of Moycullen and visited with "the local chatterbox" who knew the most about activities going on in the village. He told that person what he was doing and said, "It looks like the people in Oughterard are much more interested in going to Knock Shrine than the people here in Moycullen. Are you losing the faith here in Moycullen?" he asked.

Then he drove back to Oughterard, using his same sales pitch, only switching the place names. He told "the local chatterbox" there that the people in Moycullen seemed to be a whole lot more interested in going to Knock Shrine than the people here in Oughterard. "Are you losing the faith here in Oughterard?" he asked.

Neither town was willing to let the other get ahead of them, and it wasn't long before the lorry was full to overflowing for every pilgrimage to Knock Shrine.

Freda laughed, "They didn't have a local newspaper back then, so news was pretty much by word of mouth. It looked like he knew the right ones to tell, though."

Tim had already reflected on many of their outings, "I remember one trip when Andrew took the mass servers to Knock, and we were going up the big hill in Cornamona. He made everyone get out, then made the men push the bus up the hill. It was a very steep hill and a tall one, as well. He told the women that they must walk up the hill and re-board the bus at the top. They didn't mind doing as Andrew bid.

"It was no time at all before we had to hire a second bus," Tim repeated for emphasis, "but we always hired Andrew first."

Tim showed us a picture of one of the pilgrimage outings, which must have shown a group of 50 or 60 people gathered along the roadside. Andrew was standing right near the center of the picture, completely surrounded by his passengers — his friends and neighbors. He posed with a somber expression, but you could see by the smiles on the faces of those around him that he occupied the place of honor, while the driver and conductor of the national carrier stood to the far side of the picture like onlookers.

Freda had never seen the picture before and she enjoyed reminiscing, calling people by name. The corners of her eyes crinkled and her mouth turned up in a smile, then she said, "This is a good picture of my father." She studied the picture a little longer, saying, "He wore oversized dungarees over his pants during the week, but on Sundays he always dressed in a suit and a collar."

Hugh added, "But never a tie. Andrew never wore a tie. In fact, when he died, the photographer had to draw a necktie onto the picture that was selected for his Mass Card, because no one could find a recent picture of him wearing one."

Freda was still holding the picture, but her smile faded, she slowly shook her head from side to side and said, "He'd drive to Knock Shrine only on Sunday, through June, July and August. On 15 August, the big day in Knock, they'd all go down for the night picture, collecting the people on the way. They'd get to Knock by midnight, return home, then he'd be up at 6:00 and go with a day group. How he did it, I don't know."

No one who shared their stories seemed to be able to emphasize enough what a very gentle nature Andrew had and what a hard worker he was, working long hours. Then they never failed to add how extremely charitable he was.

Tim had told us, "He would never leave anyone on the road, whether they had the money for the fare to Knock or not.

"Another day he always attended was the Eucharist procession in Galway," Tim said. "He'd collect people around

Andrew Ferguson almost never wore a necktie. When he died, the photographer had to draw the necktie on this picture to use for his Mass card.

Collinamuck and take them in for that."

Hugh had asked Tim if Andrew ever used him as a conductor on the Pioneer Association trips. "No. We would hire the bus out and I would help with the passengers, though."

"You'd make sure that no one was left behind?" Tim nodded and Hugh laughed, saying, "I could use you on my own Connemara Bus, but it would only be a part-time job. I sometimes need help with the head count. I have trouble keeping them all together."

Hugh glanced my way with one of his warm smiles. I felt a tinge of guilt warm my cheeks, remembering how many times Hugh had to come search for me as I strayed away from the tour group.

In 1932, Andrew's business was still thriving and he saw another need to be filled, so he ordered a brand new passenger bus.

Pat O'Halloran said, "Andrew's new bus was built on a lorry chassis — a Bedford lorry chassis, it was. A coach-builder down on Foster Street in Galway built the original bus. Joe Fahy was the builder's name."

Frank O'Toole added, "The roads weren't good at that time and the lorry chassis was sturdy enough to take the hardships of the roads."

To which Pat added, "A properly designed coach would have banged up years before Andrew retired his old bus. Andrew and his brothers went to Galway city and watched them drive his new bus out of Fahy's Garage." It was not only a need well met, it was a beautiful sight to behold. The new bus was painted the color of all of Andrew's vehicles — green.

This shiny green bus enabled Andrew to drive his neighbors to the Galway city on a regular basis. It expanded their world and improved the quality of their daily lives by adding to their livelihood. The primary mission of the bus was to bring the women from Oughterard and nearby townlands and villages to Galway for market day.

The bus was officially registered as the Connemara Bus. Andrew designed the route to reach the women who lived in the isolated parts of the back roads of the parish and the bus soon became known as "Bus Na mBhan" in Irish — or "Bus of the Women" in English.

"I never helped my father drive the bus," Freda said. "The bus route started about the time I was leaving home to get married."

Andrew, along with his two brothers, Eugene and Maurice, were the only three who ever drove the first Connemara Bus. No one ever drove it but a Ferguson.

Andrew was very proud of his Bus Na mBhan, but recognized early on that it wasn't quite perfect. He and his brothers set about removing the seats that had been built in the new bus and replaced them with larger seats with more space between them. This was for the comfort of the women, who wore big red petticoats and carried large square baskets with them to market.

The red petticoats were one of the few bright spots in the dull existence of these women. For many years the petticoats were the symbol of rural and agrarian women in western Ireland. Each woman fashioned her own petticoat and dyed the wool with her best source of color, usually beet root. This gave the ladies' spirits a much-needed boost as well as a sense of style.

Not long after the trips to market became regular events, Andrew began hearing new requests from his friends and neighbors.

He didn't mind at all starting a Wednesday evening trip to bring them to Galway city to join in the excitement of the bingo games or to sip a pint in a pub. On Sunday evenings he added even more trips to the city to attend the cinema and dances, or maybe another visit to the pub. Everyone savored the taste of their new social life and thought it to be quite grand.

Before this time, it had not been possible for young people to even meet others from nearby villages. This would probably never have happened without Andrew and his Bus Na mBhan. These meetings oftentimes led to marriages.

Even Freda Ferguson met her future husband, William Ryan, at a dance in the nearby village of Moycullen. Bill had been born in Cappawhite, just outside Tipperary town in County Tipperary, but was stationed in Clifden as a policeman, or Guardian of the Peace, or Garda Siochana when spoken in Irish.

The Midland Great Western Railway, which ran between Galway and Clifden, right through the heart of Connemara, came to an end in 1935. At that time, Andrew literally was the lifeline between his parish and the rest of the world.

The demands of Andrew's growing workload could not have succeeded without assistance from his family and friends.

As Andrew's Bus Na mBhan became more important to his neighbors, it became his number one priority. Not only did the people from Coolaghy, Donlon's Cross, Oldtown, Moycullen Village, Clooniffe, and Poulnacloch come to depend on Andrew, but the bus also found more women waiting for pick-up at the Old Forge, Shrue, Birchall, Collinamuck and Tullykyne.

On Saturdays, Andrew enjoyed an occasional male passenger on the Bus Na mBhan, who usually felt more comfortable sitting or standing near Andrew's driving bench than sitting with the women, and their baskets, bundles, children and noisy poultry further back in the bus.

Andrew Ferguson's bright green Connemara Bus, 1932 Bedford-OBW, with a petrol engine, a four-speed crash-gear box, and a top speed of 37 mph.

Liam recalled, "A man named Claude Chevas, a Scotsman, used to come to Galway on a Saturday afternoon. He spoke Scots Gaelic and always wore the full Scottish national costume. In fact, he was the only man to ever wear a skirt on the Connemara Bus.

"Andrew enjoyed the company of someone to discuss world news and politics with him while the ladies visited behind them about their own weekly events."

Andrew's nephew, Henny, was the first conductor on the Bus Na mBhan. He worked right up to the time the first of Freda and Bill's three sons approached the age to serve as conductors on the bus. So Andrew created another job for Henny by starting a hackney service. Maurice helped with the taxi service a little, but mostly he was busy in his garage keeping all of Andrew's vehicles in good running order.

"Henny would go to take people home from the town of Oughterard," Freda said, "but if he wasn't about, Maurice would drive the hackney. There was always someone available to take the people where they needed to go, which was usually home from town. Up until the time Henny retired, he was still bringing people from Oughterard to their home.

"At one time, there was a local agricultural person in town, stationed in Oughterard, who didn't have a car," Freda said. "He used to hire Henny. Henny didn't have much time for his regular hackney service after that, for he was rented permanently to drive this man all over, clear to Clifden. He was an agriculture instructor — had something to do with the land, advising people how to better their land and give them advice. This kept Henny pretty busy."

Through the years, Tommy Tuck and his brother, Fay, also worked as mechanics for the bus. In fact, Tommy eventually bought the garage from Maurice. Sean Connealey also helped work on the bus. He was good about coming by for a chat to see what was the best thing to do if the bus was in need of repairs.

"My father," Pat said, "Phil O'Halloran was the carpenter who would work on the bus, and he would pull the wooden panels off to repair the frame if there was a crack or it was broken. I made sure I was always on hand to help with that job, because there were always coins to be found — coins that had been lost behind the wooden panels. I was the first one to put my hands in and get the pennies that had fallen through the cracks."

"They used a special wood on the bus, either beech or ash, and they would collect it in Galway at McDonagh's and bring it out for repairs," added Freda. "It took a lot of people to keep the old bus in running order."

However at times, Andrew would not stand still long enough to have needed repairs made — especially the radiator. Everyone laughed whenever the radiator was mentioned.

Brendan was the first to tell about the radiator.

"Andrew didn't believe in any down time, regardless how badly the bus needed repair. He used to get these tins of stuff for fixing radiators. He would pour it into the radiator. It had a picture of a seal on the outside of the can."

"Radwells," offered Hugh.

"Yes. That was it. He must have bought it by the gross," said Brendan. "Anyway, he'd put it in and it sealed up the leak for only so long, then after a few dozen cans of that, he would decide that this wouldn't do the job any longer and he would abandon it. Between here and Galway, we would have to stop about four or five times to get buckets of water to top the radiator up."

"I can still picture where he sent me to get a bucket of water at a well with briars growing in all around it. I couldn't find it, but Andrew knew it was in there. He would point and tell me, 'It's down there' and in I would go to fill the bucket."

Liam's version was, "When I was a youngster, and working as Andrew's conductor, the head gasket must have been gone or something, but the bus kept overheating. It was especially bad in the summer time. We had to get a gallon bucket and stick it inside the door of the bus. Every time we passed a well we stopped. I got to know every well from Oughterard to Galway — there must have been 30 of them. We stopped every time we passed one of them to get another bucket of water and we'd fill it up. Then when we'd stop to pick up a passenger, and we'd top off the radiator again, then drive on to the next well. So, it took us twice as long to get to Galway during that period when the radiator was giving us trouble. Needless to say, I still know and can locate every well between Oughterard and Galway.

"We stopped to get a bucket of water in Bushy Park one day. The well is still there today. It is a holy well. I think it is called, Oran's Well. There was a woman filling a bottle at the well. She said to me, 'You can't take water from that well. That's a holy well.'

"Andrew listened to the argument for a while then shouted, 'If we don't get this bus to Galway in time to pick up my passengers there will be holy bloody murder to answer to.'

"We used to stop at Christy Lydonn's shop in Knock Ferry on our way home to Oughterard on a Saturday evening — God rest Christy — a proper gentleman. On this particular day," Liam continued, "it was very hot weather and the radiator was boiling its brains out. My grandfather always bought two dozen fresh eggs off Christy and when Christy saw the radiator boiling hot, he said that a man once told him to crack a couple of eggs into it. Sure enough, we did just that. Lo and behold, the bus didn't get hot for another few days. So, on a regular basis after that, there was always a few eggs cracked into the radiator."

Brendan said, "In his later years, Andrew would put a towel or a scarf around his head and put his hat on top of it."

Hugh added, "And he would put the towel in the water bucket for the radiator, and then put it on his head to keep him cool. He would squeeze it just a little, but let it drip down on him."

"He was used to being in the Orient," Brendan said.

"He used that as his personal form of air-conditioning," Freda laughed. "It did keep him cool in the summer time."

Someone mentioned his hat again, saying, "I think his hat was older than he was." To which, another stated that he brought it with him from China.

Everyone who knew him was able to recognize Andrew from afar by his hat. Freda described his hat, saying, "It was a soft, brown felt hat. The rim was turned down all around. I thought maybe he did this when he was driving so it would shade his eyes."

Someone spoke of Andrew being the official carrier of sports teams, "He and his green bus provided the link between their side and their supporters for away-matches."

"Galway was playing Kerry," Pat said, "in the 1938 All-Ireland Final. In those days, it was quite a major event. These days, this is also true, but in those days, it was even more so," said Pat. "Andrew took a busload up to the match in Dublin, along with the team. My brother-in-law was on that trip and he told me that Andrew brought along a mechanic with him, as a safety precaution, in case there were any mechanical difficulties. It must have been some drive up to Dublin at 25 miles per hour, you know? Andrew was very careful about some parts of the mechanics of the bus.

"Andrew had his own way of caring for the bus," Pat said. "Take the battery — he would remove the battery every night. No one knew why, but he would remove it every night."

"And he would take the starter out every bloody evening," added Brendan.

Hugh asked if anyone ever saw him reverse the bus in when he went into the shed.

Pat said, "No, he'd drive it straight in. I never saw it backed in anyway."

Hugh said, "I wonder why he'd take the battery out."

Brendan added, "You know, he did this after he was getting older, and somehow he got this into his head that the battery and the starter would perform better if he did that."

"I know he was always very protective of the bus," said Hugh. "The bonnet of the old bus had a hinge in the middle of it. I was conductor on the day that Hurricane Deborah hit, in 1961. Andrew and I were trying to get into Galway on one of the first pick-up runs.

"The wind was blowing so hard and the sides of the bonnet began flapping like a big bird. The next thing we knew, Andrew and I were watching this big bonnet float away and it went about 500 yards out into the bog. I thought we were going to blow away with it. Andrew was sort of heavy at the time and I remember thinking that he was what was keeping us on the ground. I wasn't adding much weight to it at all. I gave him all of the credit.

"Andrew told me, 'We'll have to just sit here and wait, for I am too old and you are too young to go out after that bonnet.' So, we sat there for what seemed like hours. Eventually a truck came along. I think it was Dan Lydon. Dan had a rope with him and he walked over the bog, tied the rope around the bonnet and brought it back across the bog, back to the bus, and tied it on for us.

"Andrew had already made up his mind that he wasn't going to leave there without the bonnet to his bus.

"Then, we drove to a nearby house, where Andrew knew the people who lived there. He parked the bus behind the shed and we went into the house. Andrew and the couple were all talking Irish. Andrew knew Irish quite well, but he wouldn't often use it. I remember, the lady gave us a lovely bowl of stew, country butter, and brown bread.

"We waited there the rest of the day, until about 5:00, before going into Galway. The whole promenade was all broken up around the bay. Rocks were everywhere, but Andrew did not leave his people stranded in Galway. We went in to town to get them."

"People depended on him," said Frank, "and he didn't let them down. Andrew made sure he didn't let them down — ever."

"I remember one Sunday night," Pat said, "when Andrew would take the people into the pictures in Galway. One of the major stops was Moycullen, about seven miles from Galway and he would always get a good load there. He was packing them in on this night in Moycullen. He could have filled about three buses, you see, but he realized that something was funny when he spotted Tommy Watts entering for the third time. They were all coming out the back door and coming around the bus and getting on again. He could have prevented this if he had collected fares from them all, but he wasn't very much on charging them fares," Pat added. "He would sometimes get them coming off again. He wasn't much on getting the cash off anyone, you know."

"As well as that, now," Brendan said, "if Andrew thought someone was going courtin', he would wait an extra 10 minutes, or maybe 15 minutes, but if he heard someone was drinking in a pub, he'd say, 'Oh, to hell with them' and drive on without them. But the fella' who had been courtin', Andrew would say to him, 'you sit there,' and point to the front seat beside him. Andrew would keep him at the front of the bus and the fella' would be interviewed on the way out."

"It wasn't that Andrew disliked drink," Pat said, "he just wouldn't wait on them. He also wouldn't pull up and wait for guys to run into pubs. One night, he collected them at a pub and they asked him to wait just a few more minutes and he told them he wouldn't. So, someone drove a potato up the exhaust. Andrew couldn't start the engine and they got extra time in the pub anyway while Andrew diagnosed the fault. It took him maybe a half-hour or an hour to get that potato out of the exhaust. He knew who did it, all right, and he lined them up against the wall, he did, but he didn't do anything to them."

"He was a very gentle man." Liam said. "He was too soft, really. A lot of the time he knew when passengers were playing tricks on him, but he'd not mention it. The only story I ever heard about my grandfather having a side other than gentle was when I was 17 years of age," Liam continued, "I went to visit Tom Dunn and his wife in Hampshire while I was working in England. I had only met Tom once or maybe twice in my time before that. He was a very old man at the time, but he told me some lovely stories about my granddad while we were chopping wood, out in the back.

"He said the same things that everyone said about Andrew, that he was a kind and a gentle man, but Tom added a new dimension on that day. He told me that 'Andrew was a tough man as well,' he says, 'and he was always extremely fit.'

212

Daisy (Heal) Ferguson

"Tom had served with my grandfather in China, and Tom says, 'I'll never forget, we were out in the town in Shanghai. Andrew was never a drinkin' man and he got a certain amount of needlin'. You know, a little back-stabbing here and there for the Irish guys. There was always a little of that goin' on. A couple of English lads were always pickin' on the Irish guys.'

" 'One night we met up with these same lads, and I had me arm in a sling. It wasn't broken, but it was in a sling, anyway. There was a kind of a challenge between the English lads and the two of us.'

"Tom said, 'I can't help you, Andrew, with me arm in this sling.' Andrew said to never mind, 'I'll handle these two on me own.'

"Tom said, 'The next thing I knew, the two English lads were lying flat on the ground and Andrew and I was walkin' down the road together. It wasn't like Andrew at all, even though he was a tough man, it wasn't like him at all, but that night he said, 'Don't worry, I'll handle it meself — and he did."

Liam said, "I worked with my grandfather for ten years, and I never saw that side of him in my whole life — never ever. He had a temper all right, but he'd never give out to you. He was always a very gentle man."

No one took issue with Liam's claim, for they all agreed that Andrew was a gentle man as well as a gentleman.

Brendan added that as gentle as Andrew was, there was his crusty side, too.

"After Andrew's wife, Daisy, died, his priority was to keep the bus on the road at all costs. He let the pub business run down to blazes, for the simple reason that he was gone on the bus most of the time.

"Tommy Tuck had the garage next door at the time and if a charge came in and he wanted to treat him to a

People brought their animals to sell at Fair Day in the town of Oughterard, during the 1920s.

drink, he would take him next door to Andrew's pub.

"One day this guy came into the garage and he said to Tommy, 'There seems to be a problem next door in the pub.'

"Tommy said, 'Well, Andrew won't be back until late. He has gone on the bus run,' and Tommy asked the guy if he wanted to wait. So, he decided that he would wait until Andrew came back, rather than make a second call on him.

"Your Man was a health inspector.

"To fill you in on Andrew's pub, it was basically called a 'sawdust' pub. This meant that there were cement floors, and on Fair Day — particularly on a Fair Day — when people brought their animals to town for sale, you had to put down loads of sawdust. This was because all of the animals had the run of the street, with consequential muck around the place, which would then be tracked inside.

"Your Man waited all afternoon for Andrew and he came back to the pub when he returned. Your Man followed Andrew inside and introduced himself. Andrew watched him as he had a look around.

"Your Man said, 'I am afraid you will have to make a few changes.'

"Andrew asked, 'Changes? What's wrong?'

"Your Man said, 'You will have to have a toilet adjacent to the pub premises — to the public house.'

"Andrew told him he had a toilet and brought him through the kitchen and out the back door, and down the yard, and showed him where it was located — a good distance down to the end of the yard.

"Your Man looked at the 40 or 50 yards down to the back and said, 'That's not good enough.'

"Andrew asked, 'What do you mean it's not good enough?'

"Your Man said, 'It has to be adjacent to the pub.'

"Then Andrew moved a little way back up the yard and asked him, 'If I put a toilet in this room just below the turf shed, would that do?'

" 'Oh no, no, that's still too far away. It has to be adjacent to the pub.'

"Andrew tried the cow shed next, but Your Man said, 'No, that's not good enough. It must be adjacent.'

"Well, Andrew was totally ignoring this 'adjacent' business, but he was gradually and reluctantly working his way up the yard toward the pub.

"Next, Andrew tried the bottling store near the house, and Your Man said, 'No, that's still not good enough. It must be adjacent.'

"Then, Andrew tried the room that was at the back of the kitchen.

" 'No, no,' he said, 'it must be adjacent to the pub.'

"In one section of the pub there was a little window, and outside that window there was a big country tank to collect the water that came off the roof. The water was collected here and would be tapped off as required.

"By this time, Andrew was really becoming frustrated, and he said, 'If I broke a door out there and put the urinals there and a toilet over here, would that do you?'

" 'No,' he said, 'I am afraid it wouldn't be big enough.'

"Andrew said, 'What more would any man want but the width of his ass?'

"With a perfectly straight face, Your Man turned and left abruptly. He went out the door and into Tommy Tuck's garage and burst out laughing.

Tommy asked him, 'What's so funny?'

"Your Man said, 'I have to tell you this one,' and that's the way that story got told — from Tommy Tuck.

Someone asked what "the end" result was.

"The end result was that it stayed the way it was."

Roger added, "Andrew's son-in-law, Bill Ryan, nailed up a sign on the door, showing where the toilet was. And the sign read, 'This is it!' "

"Andrew's bus was always number one with him," Brendan concluded. "He would have sacrificed everything just to keep the bus on the road and his passengers content."

Roger added an amen by saying that the "Bus was the greatest thing since God made apples."

There was a general consensus that the Bus Na mBhan was the greatest thing not only for Andrew, but also for Connemara.

chapter seventeen

I HAD A DIFFICULT TIME not listing all of the times that I was told what a charitable man Andrew was. I may have left in too many of them, but I took out so many!

To again point out Andrew's charitable nature, Roger told us, "Andrew was such a great man, and a charitable man — a very, very charitable man. He never left anybody behind. If poor people wanted to go to Knock Shrine, he would take them and never charge. He would bring anyone who could not pay to Galway on the bus and not charge them. Andrew knew which person had the money and he knew the person who hadn't the money. And he had such a grand way of putting it when someone came aboard and wasn't able to pay. Andrew would say, 'You paid me before' and motion them on by him. This was his way of preserving their dignity."

Frank O'Toole agreed by saying, "He saved a lot of people. He was such a decent chap, really decent. If he thought you had it, he would take it from you, but if he thought you hadn't, he would wait. And he certainly had to wait many, many times."

Pat added, "Andrew would never charge anyone riding the bus in to Galway city to visit relatives in the hospital. I saw that myself. Many times."

Brendan said, "I remember as well, on the same subject, when I was going with him in the 1959-60 era, there was a family in Moycullen whose house burned down. From that day forward, he never charged any of that family — and they had a big family — he never ever charged them to ride the bus or any of the children."

Daisy was equally as generous, for every Friday evening she could be seen visiting more than one house with baskets of flour, tea and sugar.

Hugh said, "So many people have come up to me after I started the new Connemara Bus and told me that Daisy used to bring them food and clothing for the children, or if they were sick, she would look after them until they were well again.

"One lady from a family with eleven children stopped to talk to me as I stood beside my bus in Galway," Hugh continued. "She told me, 'Surely none of us would have lived to adulthood if it hadn't been for your grandmother's generosity.' "

Freda added, modestly, "That lady's family was only one of many that my mother helped feed. During the war, when many things were in short supply, you were much more apt to get a regular ration of tea and sugar if you were poor than if you could afford to pay. My father never questioned the loss of inventory, nor did my mother ever mention it."

"After Andrew died," Liam said, "many people came to our house and said they owed Andrew a half a crown or a ten shilling note that went back maybe 15 years. When they tried to give it to Mother, she told them, 'My father is dead and the debt died with him.' "

"I don't know how Andrew managed, sometimes." Roger added. "People only tended to pay him in the store once a year. They would run on the bill the whole year and then pay him at Christmas time when relatives sent money from the States."

Freda added, "He went on credit from his suppliers and from the bank. I remember a lot of people could not pay him and would give him a bag of potatoes or some vegetables. He might put the produce in the store to sell, or sometimes we would keep it for our own use.

"People sold their cattle only once a year. They'd come along after they'd sell their cattle and then pay their bill. They'd get credit again for as long as they needed — or whenever they'd sell their cattle again." Freda had great compassion for these people, the same as her father.

"There was no work, you see, except on the farms and sometimes some roadwork. No one had money, so I think most of the shops in Oughterard worked on credit. Then, they'd get paid when the animals were sold," she added.

Liam said, "Andrew never spoke about money. He didn't put a lot of stock in money, and he didn't really care about money. It's a bad way to be when you are in business, I suppose. He did pay me a ten-shilling note, a half a pound. He would give my pay to my mother and I got to keep the few coins that people would sometimes give me as a tip for helping them with their baskets.

"Andrew was such a hard worker, he had to eat well," Roger said. "I remember on market day, Henny O'Halloran lived next door, which was very handy for both of them, so Henny would get up and they would head out, but first Andrew would put on a fry. Anyone who worked for Andrew had to be fed first. He'd put food for them in the skillet. He'd put on a big pan of rashers, sausages, eggs, and oh, how Andrew loved gravy. He'd pour it all over everything. He would turn the pan upside down onto the plate and everything would be swimming in gravy. He was a great believer in the big breakfast."

Hugh asked Frank if he was ever a relief man for Henny. Frank said, "I was only conductor six times in me life. When it was going on to 4 o'clock, Andrew would call me when he needed me. I would go to Andrew's for breakfast, there would be, like Roger said, a pan of rashers and a pan of sausage and a pan of black puddin' and a pan of eggs. I couldn't eat half of what he gave me, but he would eat it all right. And the gravy! It was not gravy like we know gravy. His gravy was all the leavin's in the pan.

"Then, we would have to peel back, bring in turf for Andrew's mother, and we'd do the washin' up, and we would clean up everything before we left. Then, we would leave about six in the morning, go down into Collinamuck, into Moycullen, and on into Galway."

Roger said he would sometimes help Andrew as a conductor on the Sunday evening runs to go into Galway. That way Andrew would let him ride free. Roger's eyes danced as he said, "I would give them all a hand as they stumbled from the door."

Pat summed it up in a reflective way. "Andrew ran a wonderful business. He had the pub and the shop and the bus and the lorries. He ran valuable services. He drove his bus into places where the national companies, like the CIE, could not get. The people near the main road had choices of buses, but the people Andrew served had no choice. He went through the '30s and right up through the war years. It was a unique service. He was a wonderful man."

Andrew provided more than that; he was a mentor to many young people. He would be prompt to engage them in conversation, wanting to know about their plans for the future.

He was quick to encourage the young people in Connemara to speak English. He thought it was very important that they not abandon their Irish heritage, but he wanted them to become fluent and comfortable with English, in addition to the Irish language.

Brendan said, "That was the basic issue, but it went a bit deeper than that, you see. The bulk of the population of this country at that time was for emigration. At least 80-85 percent had to emigrate for work. They were going into Galway city and to English-speaking countries, like England, the United States, or some of the British colonies like New Zealand, Australia and Canada.

"I would say that Andrew's idea was that a good working knowledge of English was more beneficial than the ability to speak Irish," Brendan continued. "He'd tell them to get a good sound education on their way up — as good as possible — in the English language and mathematics and then continue to speak Irish when you are at home."

Liam said, "My grandfather would ask the parents on the bus, 'What is young Johnny or young Mary going to do when they grow up?'

" 'Oh, I don't know,' their parents would reply, 'They haven't made their minds up yet.'

" 'My advice,' Andrew would say, 'is nurses for the girls and trades for the boys.'

"And he wasn't far wrong. 'Keep away from the pick and shovel,' he'd say to me," Liam told us, laughing. "He used to drive that into my head, 'keep away from the pick and shovel,' and I have tried very hard to do that.

"Andrew got a lot of people jobs. He had a lot of contacts. It was hard to get jobs in those days, but Andrew could get the young people jobs."

Andrew Ferguson's advice was eagerly sought and closely followed. No one even suggested that he was showing any disloyalty to his heritage in giving his advice to the young people that they should speak English.

Brendan quoted him, " 'Get a good sound education on your way up — as good as possible.' Andrew wanted the best to happen to everyone and this is how he saw the needs for the future."

Each time I visit Ireland, I struggle with conflicting messages. I love to hear the lyrical lilt of the Irish as they speak, but I know that my ability to understand them is only because at one time in their history the British forced their own language upon them. The Irish learned to speak this new language only because they had to, but they retained and interjected inflections of their own Irishness into it, which my ears hear as the charm of the Irish brogue.

Especially driving through Connemara, even today you are reminded that the Irish still manage to hold a firm grip on what is their own. Proudly, Gaelic — or Irish — is seen on all of the road signs first, followed by the English translation for visitors. Their first language is still used daily in and around Connemara.

The British could not steal their language from them. They only strengthened the Irish determination to cling to what was their own, while complying with the price they were being forced to pay.

In 1843, Thomas Davis wrote in *The Nation*, "A people without a language of its own is only half a nation. A nation should guard its language — 'tis a surer barrier, and more important frontier, than fortress or river."

The Celtic circle shows no preference for one direction or the other, nor does it lean to one side or the other. This is the same with the Irish people. Both their history and occasionally their present display conflict and yet, I never fail to be aware of a tremendous sense of serenity when I am there. I proudly claim a large part of my heritage in theirs.

chapter eighteen

LIAM, WHO WORKED LONGEST as Andrew's conductor, told us, "The women in rural Ireland were very hard workers. It was considered 'woman's work' to run every facet of the home. They had to cook, bake, preserve, feed chickens, gather eggs, churn butter, make clothing, mend, wash, iron, have the children, mind the children, milk the cow, tend the livestock, and whatever else it took to make a good home.

"And it was a rule that Irish men never interfered in their woman's work.

"All the women lived hard lives. Andrew recognized this and showed his appreciation by not making things more difficult for them than they already were."

With few cars on the road from the Connemara area and no private cars at all, Andrew allowed these women to touch the outside world, even if only for a short time each week. The women appreciated what he did for them and were loyal to him. His friends and neighbors would stand out on the roadway and wave the inbound national bus to go on by them as they waited in the rain, the heat, or the cold, waiting for their beloved Bus Na mBhan. Andrew was always very protective of his women passengers and wanted their outings to be as pleasant for them as he could possibly make it.

Brendan told about Andrew sending Eugene to drive

the bus for him on one occasion.

"It seems that Andrew was ill on this particular day, which didn't happen often, for Andrew was a very healthy and hardy man. But on this day he was unable to drive the bus, so he reluctantly sent his brother in his place.

"Andrew was afraid that Eugene mightn't have the patience with the passengers that Andrew felt they deserved.

"Henny was the conductor at the time. Andrew was so very worried how the trip would go, that he was uneasy the whole time he waited. The minute the bus returned, Andrew summoned Henny. When Henny arrived at his bedside, Andrew raised up in the bed on one elbow to interview him.

"Andrew was saying to Henny, 'How did Eugene get on?' "

" 'Oh, grand, grand,' replied Henny.

" 'How did he treat the passengers?'

" 'Oh, fine, fine,' Henny said, nodding his head.

" 'Did he use any bad words?'

" 'No. No, he didn't, Andrew,' Henny said, shaking his head.

" 'Are you sure he didn't?'

" 'No, he didn't.' Henny tried to reassure Andrew that Eugene hadn't used any bad language, but Andrew was hard to convince.

"Henny finally succeeded in reassuring him and Andrew eased back in his bed and rested for what was probably the first time that day. He was finally convinced that Eugene had properly cared for the passengers on his Bus Na mBhan."

"Andrew was the first licensed private operator in Oughterard, so there was only his bus and the national company," Hugh said. "There weren't that many buses on the road, anyway, but Andrew's bus was the only bus that came off of the main road to serve these people."

There was an apparent difference in the way each participant remembered the bus route itself, so we deferred to Liam's memory, since he worked the longest as bus conductor.

Hugh and Liam drove me through the back roads to show me Andrew's bus route. This was a very generous thing for them to do, and I appreciated it, but I would have preferred they not have driven the route backwards. I guess they didn't realize how easily I get confused. I have tried to reverse it to its proper order. If I got confused, I apologize.

"We would come down to Galway on our regular route first thing in the morning," said Liam. "The first crossroad on the route was called Old Forge, because at one time there actually was an old forge there. The name still hangs on. The area was very remote. Not as many houses as there are now. It was down here that Andrew would get the bulk of his passengers. They all looked forward to Saturday. They loved their Saturday Bus Na mBhan.

"I don't remember all of the ladies' names. Back then, you would not call them by their first name. It was always Mr. or Mrs. and then you used their surname." Liam chuckled and said, "We had more manners than we do today.

"Most of the passengers were older ladies who, almost without exception, wore shawls, long flannel skirts that barely brushed the tops of their black or brown lace-up boots.

"They carried baskets of fresh hen eggs and duck eggs, fresh-baked soda bread and brown bread, homemade jams, home-churned butter. They would finish off the top of their butter with their own fancy designs, then wrap it in cabbage leaves, put it in a bucket, and drop it down in the well to harden for the trip. They would bring hand-knit socks and sacks of live chickens and ducks — all being carried to market.

"Around the holidays, they also brought their prized geese and turkeys. Helping the ladies aboard with their parcels, bundles, wicker baskets and livestock was the conductor's job.

"As we traveled toward the Galway market, the women with their baskets of eggs would gather near the back bench and strive to even-out their quantities. They wanted to see that as many as possible had at least a score — eggs were sold then by the score instead of the dozen or half-dozen. When they arrived at the market, each had as close to the same number as could possibly be divided, even if they exceeded the score. They all understood that hens are a lot like people and don't always do what is expected of them, so when these times visited, they could rest assured that the others would help them until their own hens start to lay again.

"They depended on this income to buy their staples that would see them through the coming week. Each of them looked out for their neighbor, just as they did for themselves. I especially remember Mrs. Osbourne. She was a great traveler on the bus."

Liam stopped talking as though lost in thought. He smiled, then added, "Those were different times, really."

"There was a gravel road at that time and very little traffic. You would seldom meet anybody. People did not drive as fast, either. If you did come across somebody you had plenty of time to negotiate or reverse up. Somebody had to give way — the roads were very narrow. When Andrew and I would travel the road, we'd maybe meet two or three cars all day. We'd travel maybe 15 or 20 miles without seeing a car.

"The next area was Shrue, coming into Berchall. We used to pick a lot of our passengers up from along there.

We might get an occasional man, but not many. It was mostly women.

"They all had big families as well. There were no small families, all six children and upwards. Big families and small houses, everybody was the same. They all needed feeding and looking after. There was one thing about those in the farming business, you might never have any money in your pocket, but you had something to eat, fresh eggs, fowl, and grew your own vegetables, so they were rich in that way. It was a nice family life that you could not put a price on really.

"Two of the younger women were Winnie Sweeney and Kit Carter. Both are still living in Collinamuck. They were both great lovers of the bus.

"Every Saturday Winnie would ride on the bus and at that time she was in her 20s and most of the others were older women. She would tell them about being out dancing the night before, and tell about her boyfriends.

"Before the bus, the people at that time had no way of getting to town. They used to meet at the crossroads. You might get 40 or 50 people to meet here in Collinamuck Cross. They had very little money. They would stand around and have a chat and this is where 'Dancing at the Crossroads' came from. The people would dance to the music of a céilí band on a summer evening.

"Particularly in the area where the bus traveled, the women looked forward to a day out to go into Galway on a Saturday. You could tell the way they acted on the bus. When they got on, they all had their own little stories. And Winnie would entertain the older women with hers. They liked this.

"The women could not have met other people from the local areas if they hadn't had the bus. People from five or six miles away would not have met back then, except maybe at a funeral. They met and got to know each other, and were soon on first-name terms. They would have a bit of a chat and a bit of a craic (fun) among themselves.

"The next townlands were Knockferry and Burnt House, then Park and Wormhole. After that came the village of Gortmoor, probably hit severely by famine, which is how its name came about. The place of the 'big hunger.'

"The straight road up there was Pollnacloch," Liam recalled. Pollnaclock is the area on the road up to Barna. It is known as being the 'hole in the stone' in English.

"Andrew would park just across the road here and he'd look up that road for his passenger. I don't remember her name, but I remember she wore a black shawl. You'd see her way up that road, maybe a quarter to half a mile up and he'd send me up to help her down with her baskets. He couldn't drive up there, because there was no way to turn around. Andrew'd sit here maybe 10, 15 minutes, putting him way behind schedule, but that didn't matter."

Andrew's bus followed a schedule — sort of. On the in-bound trips to market, every person knew when the bus was suppose to arrive at their stop, but if Andrew must wait five or ten minutes on one of them to gather her belongings, or tend to some other last minute matter, he willingly waited. And she knew he would. By the time he continued to do this at every other stop down the road, they would arrive in Galway, maybe an hour late — sometimes more. No one ever minded waiting on the bus, because they knew Mr. Ferguson would also wait on them, if need be.

"Just before the hill, that next house was Sheila Herney.

"It was a major negotiation getting the bus up the hill with a busload of women. Low gear all of the way up. I used to say me prayers before we'd go up. These hills were big hills for a small lad. Not so big now, but they were at that time. When we approached the Moycullen hill, I used to break out into a sweat with fear."

"When we came to the village of Moycullen," Hugh interjected. "The bus had to negotiate a big hill with a full load. That is where we would get out and put the stone in behind the wheels. Andrew's handbrake wasn't working. To get to the top of the hill, we'd have to jump out, get a stone from the top of the wall, put it back behind the back wheel. He'd let off the foot brake, put it into first gear, then, he'd pull forward and I'd move the stone back to its place, jump back on the bus and away we would go. That stone was there for years — the same stone. Liam used it, I used it, and probably Connie and Henny before us."

"A very well known character lived down that road. The cottage is in ruins now. Martin Lydon a very well known horseman. People used to run horses and he would look after them. He was a blacksmith as well. His mother used to come on the bus with us. She was a lovely lady.

"One of the greatest characters to ever come on the bus was Mrs. Tierney," Liam said. "Very old lady. She smoked a pipe — a clay pipe. She's long gone now.

"All of the ladies had baskets — huge baskets. I wasn't able to lift Mrs. Tierney's baskets. They were too heavy. We would hold onto the handle, each. These ladies were very strong people.

"There were few houses down there. The next stop was Mom Laffey's in Tullykyne. She had a brown shawl and a black shawl," Liam remembered. "Every Saturday she would change shawls. Even though she had a big family, she would give me a three pence piece every Saturday. That was a big tip, really. She would give me that for helping her on with the bags and the baskets. She lived to be in her 90s. She had relations in America, as well. Everybody around here had relations in America."

Once Liam started working as Andrew's conductor, he

worked every Saturday year-round and every Wednesday when he was on holiday from school. On Saturdays, he and his grandfather must make several round-trip pick-ups to accommodate all of the passengers.

"We would crawl out of bed around 5 a.m. to bring their scheduled 7 a.m. run straight to Galway, then return to the more out-of-the-way roads for more passengers. We made three and sometimes four trips to Galway. It would be late morning before we gathered everyone from all the different by-ways of Connemara and transported them.

"The passengers had a week's worth of living to exchange with their friends and neighbors. So, between the visiting women, the chatter of the children, the racket of the poultry, the grinding of the gear-box, and the hum of the bus engine and the rest of its running parts, it was always a noisy trip to Galway, but everyone enjoyed it.

"On the return trips, the bus started with a pick-up at Collinamuck at 3 p.m. to gather day-old chicks and what a lovely noise they did make! Then, throw in a few live banbh (piglets) with the baby circe (chicks) and the lovely noise advances to a plain racket. Muslin sacks of flour and bran were loaded on to the top of the bus, along with a few needed provisions for Andrew's own shop. This was loaded up ahead of the passengers and then all would be delivered back to their homes, and sometimes even to the homes of neighbors who didn't make the trip. Another sort of delivery service, if you will."

Liam related an errand he was expected to run for his own friends. "Each of these young, red-blooded Irish lads knew, either from the occasional movie they attended, or from what someone related — someone who had attended, that Hopalong Cassidy ate "Spangle Sweets" on a regular basis. And these lads all coveted their own weekly ration."

Knowing that Mr. Ferguson rested at either his daughter's

or his brother's house in the afternoons, they depended on Liam to make a run to the Woolworth store during that time to buy the prescribed number of sugar-sweets needed to fill orders along the return route. Liam, like his grandfather, also filled a vital role in the enrichment of the lives of his friends and neighbors.

When the passengers begin boarding for the return trip, new pots and pans were placed under the seats as the ladies held their china and other breakables in their laps. They waited while Andrew and Liam tossed their purchases of machinery repair parts and other large items onto the roof rack of the bus.

The same white muslin sacks from the flour and bran served many needs. They were hemmed and used as dish towels, or became material for hand-sewn shirts. For an inbound bus trip, on the way to market, a yet-to-be-transformed sack would provide a temporary use by pulling it up over the body of ducks or geese, then tying it off around their necks, exposing only their heads. The ladies held their wiggly cargo in their laps.

Coming up on Christmas in the early 1940s, one of Andrew's best customers sat with her prized goose on her lap, heading for the Galway Market. A young fellow sitting on the seat beside his mother was having a difficult time resisting the temptation to turn and look at the muslin-encased goose behind him. He grabbed the back of his seat to assist him in the twist-around and quick as a blink, the goose nipped him on the finger. The young lad let out a holler that seemed to greatly exaggerate the depth of his injuries.

When his crying failed to subside, Andrew pulled the bus off to the side of the road and lifted his big frame out of the driver's seat to investigate the cause of the ruckus. Andrew picked up the lad's hand, looked at it, laid it back down, then turned to his passenger and asked, "Is the goose all right?" His passenger affirmed that the goose seemed to be doin' just fine, so Andrew returned to his driver's bench, ground the bus into gear, and continued on down the road with no further complaints from the young man.

chapter nineteen

HUGH FINALLY GOT HIS OPPORTUNITY to be the conductor of the Connemara Bus when Liam went to work in England. Hugh never had to step aside for Anthony, for he held the job as conductor until his grandfather's retirement, at the age of 79.

On the 17th day of October 1964, *The Galway Observer* printed, "The end of the line for the Connemara Bus. The famous green bus owned by veteran Mr. Andrew Ferguson of Main Street Oughterard has come to the end of the line! The roads around the lake, the main Oughterard/Moycullen/ Galway Road will no longer see the bus, which has been bringing the country folk and their produce from their homes to the city and back for 32 years. Oughterard will see little of 79 year-old Andrew Ferguson, for the kindly man is moving into Woodquay, in Galway to live with his daughter, Freda."

Andrew was quoted as saying he never had a bad passenger and never had one act of vandalism to the bus. He had many a wild young lad aboard, but he always let them have their fling, and to wherever he transported them, they knew he would wait on them until they were ready to come home (unless they were too long in a pub).

It was a sad day for Connemara when Andrew retired his Connemara Bus. It was a well-known fact that in all of those 640,000 miles, he was very proud that he never failed to complete a journey and the old bus still didn't have a scratch on it, except from an occasional tree limb or maybe some brambles.

When Andrew was asked what he would do with the bus, he said he thought it would make such a good show-piece for the Bedford people, they should buy it for their museum.

No one seemed to remember what actually became of the old bus.

Thirty years later, Hugh purchased a bus quite similar to his grandfather's old one and began reliving the journey from his past for the pleasure of sharing it with tourists.

His brother, Anthony, and sister-in-law, Sally, found the vintage bus for him in England, near Dover. Hugh designed the new route to best display the traditions and customs of Connemara, and where possible, traveled the same routes that his grandfather had gone with the original bus.

On Saint Patrick's Day in 1995, Hugh introduced the re-creation of Andrew Ferguson's Connemara Bus route. The rain, hail, and gale-force winds did not keep friends, neighbors, and admiring strangers away, nor were anyone's spirits dampened by the inclement weather. Many turned out to celebrate the return of their beloved Connemara Bus in the St. Patrick's Day Parade in Galway city.

Following the parade, the bus made its way back to Oughterard to be met by another crowd of friends and neighbors who had come from local parishes and congregated on the square of this quiet little village. Some were dressed in period clothing, some took their first ride on the new bus and some came to exchange interesting family tales about the old bus.

In preparation for this great event, a Galway radio

station invited Freda and her two sons to be guests on a talk show, to be interviewed about the new Connemara Bus, and to reminisce about the old bus.

While they were talking, the young lad who had been bitten by the goose called in and identified himself as such. He claimed that he still bore the scar on his index finger, where the goose nipped him.

He visited on the airwaves for quite a long while and told about another time he remembered riding the bus, "Andrew was driving the bus near Tullykyne and the track rod end came loose from the bus, and when the track rod went, the wheel turned into the ditch. A man driving a steam engine with a wench on it was nearby, working for the Council. He pulled the bus out of the ditch and got the bus back on the road. This man then took part of the steam engine and stuck it in where the track rod should be and he tied a bicycle tube around it and Mr. Ferguson went off with the bus and did six or seven more runs that day."

The caller also told about the radiator boiling over.

"Mr. Ferguson would stop to get water and top off the radiator. One day, he asked me to get out and do this for him and when I did it, I put the radiator cap in me pocket while I was completing the job. I still have the radiator cap from Mr. Ferguson's old bus. And if Mr. Ryan would like to have the old radiator cap, I will give it to him."

Hugh told me, "This man did come to me in the city one day and identified himself. He offered to give me the radiator cap, but I told him to keep it along with his memories of my grandfather."

I, too, have received magnificent gifts to keep along with my memories of Hugh's grandfather.

I looked around the table at the friends and family of Andrew Ferguson, and felt as if I was a part of this beautiful Irish family.

I have fulfilled my secret dreams of coming home to Ireland.

In the beginning, I wrote, "I carry a secret dream to walk barefoot through a field of wildflowers, pace my stride and sway to the roar of the sea, fill my lungs with the earthy smell of burning turf swirling from the chimney of a nearby cottage. I want to get to know an Irish family and experience a portion of their tenderness as they wrap their arms around me and embrace me. I want to listen to the warmth of their soft-spoken brogue, peppered with humor and song."

I have indeed done all of these things. I have walked through my field of wild flowers, though not barefoot — yet. I have paced my stride and swayed to the roar of the sea. This refreshes me and softens my hard edges like the brush of an angel's wing on my cheek. I have filled my lungs with the earthy smell of burning turf every time Hugh and Debbie invited me to their home for a meal. A visit always includes a meal. They are yet to fail having a turf fire burning for me.

The Fergusons and the Ryans have indeed wrapped their arms around me and embraced me. And believe me there is always an abundance of soft-spoken brogue, peppered with humor and song.

I was invited to tea one afternoon at Liam and Maura's home and Liam played his fiddle for me. What a treat!

Roger Finnerty asked if I felt like I had been adopted into the family. My eyes brimmed with tears and I could not answer him. Hugh's wife, Debbie, replied, "I am sure she does, but she hasn't decided yet whether she wants to be a Ryan or a Ferguson."

There were many hugs as I offered my thanks to each of them and especially to Freda for allowing me to share her life and her father's beloved Bus Na mBhan.

epilogue

ON SEVERAL OCCASIONS, Hugh and his mother, Freda, have both unknowingly preceded sentences with, "Now that you are back home ..." or on the telephone it is, "When you come back home. ..." My writing skills are not adequate to express the feelings that well up in me when I hear these words.

All along, I have not felt as if I had the right to financially benefit from such a wonderful solution to my own personal problems. I struggled at length with how to keep the proceeds of this book in Connemara.

After many hours of sharing and planning, Hugh, Debbie and I came up with a business plan that will fund a cottage industry in the Connemara community.

I will make periodic trips "back home" to help steer the business and visit my new Irish family.

My prayer is that God will enrich your life as much as He has blessed mine.

ORDER FORM

This book is the perfect gift.

Please send _____ copies of

"The Connemara Bus"

Name _____

Address_____

City/State/Zip _____

Each book is priced $14.95 plus $4.00 for sales tax, packing and shipping. Enclose check (payable to Leathers Publishing) or indicate credit card information.

Bill my: ☐ Visa   ☐ MasterCard

Card No. _____ Exp. Date _____

Your Signature _____

Use this form or photocopy and mail to:
Leathers Publishing
4500 College Blvd., #180
Overland Park, KS 66211

For information, call (913) 498-2625
Fax order to (913) 498-1561